**ANDY PRICE & SIMON YOUNG**

# BULLSH*T, PRIVA
# VIDEOS AND YOUTUBE MARKETING.

# ANDY PRICE & SIMON YOUNG

# BULLSH*T, PRIVACY, TOASTERS, VIDEOS AND YOUTUBE MARKETING.

**Everything you ever needed to know about the bullsh*t in marketing and why YouTube is ace.**

Copyright © Simon Young & Andy Price, 2021
Published: September 2021 by FCM Publishing
paperback: 978-1-914529-14-6
ebook: 978-1-914529-15-3

All rights reserved.
The right of Simon & Andy to be identified as the authors of this Work has been asserted by them in accordance with sections 77 and 78 of the Copyright, Designs and Patents Act 1988.
No part of this publication may be reproduced, stored in retrieval system, copied in any form or by any means, electronic, mechanical, photocopying, recording or otherwise transmitted without written permission from the publisher. You must not circulate this book in any format.

Copyright of all illustrations and imagery used within remains solely with their originator. No breach of copyright is implied or intended and all material is believed to be used with permission. Should you feel that your copyright has been impinged, please contact the publisher to ensure appropriate acknowledgment may be made.

Cover Design by Andy Price
Type Design by Red Cape Production, Berlin

# Table of content

▶ **Foreword**  9

▶ **Introduction**  13
Jeff, Mark, Steve, Tim, Sundar, Bill and all those guys  13

▶ **About The Authors**  17
Simon  17
Andy  19

▶ **Writing this book**  25
Simon  25
Andy  28

▶ **The History of YouTube | Simon**  33

▶ **The Agency Landscape | Simon**  41
Those that DO and those that talk  43
Laziness in Advertising, what's gone wrong  44
Is Facebook dead and saturated with Ads, what & where next for FB?  48
What's that WhatsApp  52
Reach Various Audiences on different platforms & devices  55
Overcharging—The 'pay per lead' model  56
Overcharging—The retainer model  62
Where the future of ads lie  64

▶️ **Social Media | Simon**  69
Addicted to Social Media?  73

▶️ **Building a brand | Andy**  79
First, what is a brand?  80
Selling propositions  83
Using emotion  92
Understanding our customers  96
Truth in ads  101
Why creativity is key  104
Why it's authentic and the way forward for ALL brands and business  108
What's your customer thinking?  110
Your Domain, value in the brand (putting it on the balance sheet)  114

▶️ **SEO | Simon**  121
SEO is brand  121
A little knowledge  132
Where does this leave us? Well...  134
A clean-up is in order  134
SO, what's the future for SEO  135
Edutainment  139

▶️ **Video Killed the ********* | Simon**  143
How did YouTube gain its advantage?  145
What wins on YouTube  146
The Barriers to Entry—Beware  149
A picture paints a thousand words. So, what does video do?  162
What are Video Views Worth  165

Mission, Vision and Values. Why they are key
to nail, especially on YouTube   167
Answer Engines and video answers   168
Growing your channel   173
Placing videos into search results   176
Ranking Videos and the new world of SEO
(search engine optimisation)   188

▶ **Technical shit and the boring
chapter (nerdom) | Simon**   193
Some of the basics of YouTube Ads   193
What should your initial goals be for your
campaigns?   207
Letting Google Learn   209
The Importance of Tracking   211
Building exclusion lists   217
It's not all about ROAS or the initial profitability   219

▶ **An introduction to how to approach
YouTube Ads | Simon**   223
Some YouTube Advert Formats to choose from   223
How to structure your approach to YouTube Ads   228
Once you are a winner   235
Routine makes a massive difference   239

▶ **Conversion Diagnostics | Simon**   245
Letting the Algorithm Learn   247
View-Through and Analytics   251
Pixels, tracking   260
Stopping Fraudulent Clicks   268
The Audience Manager   275

▶ **What Google knows about you | Simon**  285
Google knows EVERYTHING about you and who you are  285
They are ALL listening—is that right, or fair?  286
Your privacy and the aluminium helmet brigade  290
Fraud and Google—Clicks from bots and other scandalous underhand practices  295
The Poachers Turned Gamekeepers  299

▶ **Some helpful bits and bobs | Andy**  305
Video production values  305
The Customer Avatar (or Profile as I prefer)  317
Definition of target audience  318
Types of target audience  319

# ▶ Foreword

▶ I remember it clearly. A conversation with a friend of mine, Steve Qualye. More of a catch up than a conversation. Steve is one of the best sales trainers in the game and he was proudly showing me a video testimonial from a mutual friend, Bob Proctor. A legend in personal growth and a star of the hit movie 'The Secret.' I was pleased for Steve, he deserved it but just as we were signing off, he gave what could only be described as a throw away comment that went like this...

*"Hey Pete, not sure if your ads are going OK on social but there's a couple of guys out there you really should connect with. They're wizards and doing real magic for some people I know."*

Steve knew me well. As a seasoned entrepreneur I was always open to, and valued, good connections. Especially ones that could impact the bottom line of the business.

*"Sure, shoot me an intro."*

I threw back as we finished the call. Little did I know then that the 'Wizards' he was talking about, Simon and Andy, were senior graduates of the Hogwarts school of Ad Magic. Minus the pointy hats and wands. It turns out the magic they bought was in a formula. One that neither of them on their own could have created. Kind of a witches brew. It just worked. It was synergistic. Symbiotic.

One of those one plus one equals eleven deals. Like one of those cocktails you experiment with at a party that shouldn't taste great but does, even though you could never quite figure out why.

There are several parts so let me share with you some of the main parts of the recipe (you'll read about the rest later). First, we take one part Simon. Old school self-confessed lifelong geek. A veteran of the web in every sense. Combine that with a passion for analysing data, looking for patterns, spotting trends, seeing things from angles most people never think of and you have a pretty potent base ingredient. Next, we add Andy. A brilliant marketing mind who's been the brains and backbone behind some of the most successful brands and campaigns in the business. So far so good.

But next comes the real secret sauce. Both of them saw what many missed or ignored. That while Facebook was getting all the attention, there was a platform that had become the second largest search engine in the world, owned by the biggest business and they were able to combine that using their powerful algorithms to strategically target people in a way Facebook could never do. Yes, we are talking about YouTube.

Knowing how to crack THAT code is a combination lock to millions in profits and scaling your business to the moon. And these guys have cracked it. And so much more. Finish off with the umbrella in the glass of a strong commitment to the client, a passion for results and an unwavering dedication to keep pushing the boundaries of what's possible and you have a spell that can bring life, positioning, visibility and, of course, profitability to virtually any business in any niche on the planet. I've now had the pleasure of working with both of these guys for nearly two years and I am thrilled to write the foreword to this book as within its pages lies all of their genius for you to see. I also know that if you spend one cent on advertising without reading and digesting this book, you are leaving money on the table. And most likely a fortune.

Trust me, it's not often a book like this comes along because it's not often the planets align to bring you the magic these guys have found together. But when it does it's time to smile, get focused and dive in with both feet, notepad set. When I had that first conversation with Steve, I was spending around five grand a month on ads. Now I'm happily spending over a hundred. You can do the math. All I know is I was very happy with the introduction and so will you be. So go get your wizards hat ready as the magic is about to start.

**Peter Sage**
International No.1 Best Selling Author
Teacher, Trainer & Coach.
Instagram petersage007

# ▶| Introduction

**Jeff, Mark, Steve, Tim, Sundar, Bill and all those guys**

▶ Everything. Everything is analysed and recorded. We have to admit that through the 'Internet of Things' (IOT), from the books you are reading, to the websites you visit and the things you buy, we are all being monitored for our every move. The conversations we have on the phone, or just those that are within an earshot of a device, even our so-called 'private' banking data is all far from being just that—private. That is not being questioned. The point is where does that stop? We will get to the point, if we are not already there to some extent, where you buy something and you don't even know why!

Andy and I have both gone through the Elite Mentorship Forum; this is a training course by Peter Sage. I could talk about Peter's work for hours, but to keep it brief, Peter is a renowned entrepreneur, motivational speaker and most of all, a huge inspiration to those who are looking to make it in the online world. The bottom line for me is the power of positivity and the fact that what you think about yourself personally reflects in your outer world. I'd like to say we can both count Peter among our circle of friends now, having worked with him and for him over the last couple of years. Peter avoids the media, he believes that watching news is a waste of your time and cannot have a positive impact on your life. He refers to the television as the 'electronic income reducing machine' and it's true to a great extent. The more crap you take in, the more rubbish you believe, and that changes your outlook and ultimately influences your way of life, happiness, love, relationships, and so on.

Apply what Peter teaches. There are many other experts out there saying similar things on social media. It's easy to see that younger people are being herded into behaviours that they would not normally be practicing, if it were not for the endless stream of influence from the so-called 'influencers' of today. I'm also a follower of Simon Sinek, the British born, American motivational speaker. If you get a chance to watch some of his talks about how the internet and social media are changing our culture, I would highly recommend it. In summary, it's not the fault of younger generations who have only grown up with the internet in their lives and know nothing different, it's not their fault that the expectation of an immediate like or some form of affirmation is now built into the way people think. It's spreading fast—even my 70 year old mother had a go at me the other week for not liking a few of her Facebook posts. She said to me *"Why haven't you liked the last couple of posts I put up on Facebook, was there something wrong with them?"*

...WOW, those were words I never thought my mum would utter, but this is the world today! My answer to her concerns was something along the lines of, *"Yes I saw the posts but just because I've not liked them doesn't mean I dislike the post!"* Nowadays it is almost seen as an offence to not take the time to click the 'like' button on the posts of close friends or family. As with the proof right here, I was now feeling the scorn of my own mother over a few Facebook posts! I feel like we are promoting a 'like based culture' wherein, if you aren't seen to like the person on social media, then your relationship in the real world can be affected.

Is that the culture we are living in right now? This seems to me like it's a dangerous route to be going down. I feel extremely privileged to have grown up without the internet, with it getting going as I started my career and seeing it develop. I'm also lucky that I became obsessed with search engines, ads and everything 'internet' at a point in my life where I could dedicate most of my free time to learning. As a society though, we have to question where this will all end up, maybe we are already in 'The Matrix' and it's all too late, LOL! :)

I'm Simon Young and along with my business partner Andy Price, we have between us notched up a combined 50 years in marketing, branding, eCommerce, social media and have ran several agency level brand campaigns. I've been described as one of the OGs in Search Engine Optimisation (SEO)/Social having worked on the internet since its very beginnings. Andy himself is one of the original 'mad men' having been Creative Director at a few of the biggest agencies outside of London and has worked on many national brands. I guess what I'm saying is, we've seen a lot of the good times and not so good times in marketing. We run a specialist YouTube Ads agency together with a team of enthusiastic and talented people—that's s.media.

Working together over the last 2 years, we created what was to be trademarked as our Intelligence Driven Advertising Results (IDAR®) system. A mixture of our experience, tech, AI, creativity and data insight, the system went on to produce results, many of which were unexpected and huge learning opportunities and others that achieved 10,000%+ Return on Investment (ROIs). We knew they were really onto something special. The system was born out of some crazy campaigns on the Google Display Network. Let's say something about the display network first, it consists of pretty much anywhere on the internet or anything connected to it. Extreme care has to be taken on placement choice. In one infamous example, I managed to spend over £3000 of a client's budget within 24 hours and delivered half a million web visitors to their website. Blind panic ensued when the client phoned and asked what the hell was going on? He'd had orders, but far more than he could produce.

The point being, there are some amazing opportunities with display, but there are a million other chances to blow the budget with a click of a mouse. Therefore, 99% of Pay per Click (PPC) experts would most likely tell you that display is a waste of time, even those in the 1% would most likely take the safer routes to conversions and those that involve less work, testing and learning.

Being there at the inception of the internet has been an advantage. ∎

# ▶ About The Authors

 **Simon**

▶ I often describe myself as a 'web dinosaur', having roamed the bleak wilderness of what was pre-Google for nearly 10 years, building sites and ranking them. I've worked on the web pretty much every day since its inception, but let's go back to the beginning of my journey. Having been given a ZX Spectrum as a Christmas present back in the early 80s and being a proud owner of a BBC Micro, and then an Olivetti, I'd started off programming basic instructions back when it all had to be saved on floppy disks. I'd suffered the connectivity issues and frustrations of a 56k dial up connection (several hundred times slower than speeds are today), but the bleep sounds and the stripes up the sides of the screens as games loaded were nice. Those were the games that came on a cassette tape. Please don't stop reading if you haven't got a clue what I'm on about, bob on over to YouTube and search 'ZX Spectrum loading games' and you'll see what I mean. Those were the days!

So, having been born right at the right time for the evolution of computing, I became fascinated. For those of you that don't understand this, imagine a world without computers or the internet and then see yourself as a 13 year old boy who gets to play a computer game for the first time, eyes wide open and no going back—MAGIC.

Over time, I found I could get people to read pages of mine all over the world just by getting a few words in the right places. I'm mildly autistic (whatever that means), despite failing an official diagnosis. But having spent quite a lot of time in the presence of behaviourists and psychologists, I appear to have many of the characteristics associated with autism. I got sucked into the matrix that is the World Wide Web (www.) from day one, obsessing over search engines until the early hours of the morning for years on end.

I've worked through the frustrations of running businesses and working on national brands' social media accounts, where I've felt handcuffed by 'corporate say-so's' (the 'this is the way we have always done it' and 'my way or the highway' people), to now bring all that experience together on a tightly focused niche; running campaigns that literally a handful of people worldwide can say they would be comfortable with. Now that's really exciting!

There are not many people out there with the depth of experience in PPC, display, conversion diagnostics, strategic SEO and keyword intent with a business background as a former accountant as me. I've done all the 'naughty stuff'—been in the dark web, the black hat techniques, and at one time I was one of the biggest spammers in the world. I've cheated, schemed, written the code, link farmed, mass content spinner, auto commenter, scraper and everything in between! Of course, that was way back in the past!

I now have a passion to be authentic online, to teach people the power of social selling and to help those concerned with social media privacy. I'm a snowflake educator, a human lie detector, conversion diagnostic enthusiast and data analyst. I'm fascinated with answer and search engines—basically caught up in the web and the marketing possibilities of audience design and manipulation, almost caught up in the power of euro-Linguistic Programming (NLP) and a believer in the impossible.

Wow, I just typed that and now I sound like a massive prick, LOL! I think I'm actually a nice, honest guy, very principled and I can sleep well at night. I'm a family man with a passionate gritty northern wife who is the educator hero to my three kids, lover of the outdoors, comedy and fishing. I want to help as many people as I can, do good—if only there were more time.

I could have been a millionaire if I was bent over many times and hadn't lost everything more than once. Now I am much calmer and focused, age and experience eventually came good. I was focused and on a mission to drive ethical advertising through data—then I met Andy, he's got the bits 'Mr Technical' is missing, he's the Picard to my Data.

**Andy**

I'm the opposite of Simon.

When I was a kid, I was always outside playing football in the park. All hours. On the bike. Pop up lollies and dirty knees.

Not a PC in sight.

I was once offered a PC at Christmas (when my parents had a bit of cash). The choice was between a pool table from Intersports (remember them?) or a console. It was either the Spectrum or Commodore. All my mates had these new-fangled PC games thingy mawhostsits. I played them and liked them, but didn't really get them.

So, I opted for the pool table.

I guess I wasn't really a nerd.

When not playing pool and footy in the park, I'd build crazy shit with Lego and draw pictures of madcap cars.

You see where this is going?

I was pretty much useless at most things. I wasn't the brightest and had to work very hard to get my base GCSEs (which I did). However, Art was my love. I loved the graphics side and that's what I ended up doing. Right brain as opposed to left brain.

I didn't do the degree bit. One of the best courses in the UK wasn't a degree but a HND at Stockport College. So I opted for that.

I moved from the design side to the advert side halfway through and ended up leaving Stockport with a job. The job was at BRAHM, one of the best agencies in the north. Looking back, it was brilliant, and I learned a lot from some

## About The Authors

very talented people. It felt like the back end of the Madmen days. It was a bit of 'sex, drugs and rock and roll' in the feel and attitude of the company. But compared to what most of my mates were doing it was in fact a bit more glamorous. It was the end of the 80s and I was taught the craft of old school advertising. TV, Radio, Print, posters and press. I loved picking up a blank layout pad and marker pen. We didn't even have Macs on our desks! Friday lunchtimes at the pub were frequent, great parties at award shows were all good fun too. I won plenty of awards and generally had a fantastic time.

I spent the best part of nearly 30 years playing the game of old school ad man. It had changed. The rise of Direct Message (DM), the fall of DM, web, social and Google all came in. The old stuff has gone away a little. It's still here but not in the same way.

But one thing I would say. The craft and skill of producing great ads is still just as relevant, if not more so today. Why?

Because most of the communications out there are dog shit. Irrelevant. Twaddle. Poor. Banal.

And if we are to stand out (for the right reasons of course) in today's bloated, message-filled world, we need great ideas that resonate with customers more than ever before.

So, my old school ways and skills are perfect for today's transient world of marketing.

I had a weak spot though in my early 40s. The dirty world of digital (I say that because I didn't understand it!).

I wrote on my business plan (a 10 year plan if you remember Tony Brooks?) that I would need to merge, buy or get bought by a digital company and that I really needed to understand it more.

Well, fast forward to year 6 and my old agency doesn't exist, I merged, and set up a new one. Little did I think when I met Simon, that we would end up where we are today (I thought he was a bit special back then!).

But we have, and it's bloody brilliant. As he said, he's Data!

A true genius in the matrix.

Despite that, where the magic happens is the collision of the two worlds. Great ideas and targeting in ways like never before.

Happy days. ∎

# ⏭ Writing this book

## Simon

▶ Although this book has been a pain, it's also something I've wanted to do for a very long time. They say there is a book in all of us!

When I first spoke to Taryn Johnston (our publisher) I told her I was definitely not a reader, let alone a writer.

In fact, I said to Taryn, *"What I am about to tell you will either shock, surprise or horrify you."*

First you have to realise that books are more than just a passion for Taryn. If you want to watch her TEDx talk titled 'ced and shocked that she didn't even ask me what those two books were.

So, initially, with that admission made, I felt like I had very little chance, or right to actually get a book into print. Then I went on to tell the story of why.

You see, when I was in my first year of middle school (so I think I would have been 10 at the time) I was caught chatting in the back of the class, while I should have been paying attention.

The teacher took me to the front of the room and gave me a book. I can't remember what it was, it was opened swiftly to a chapter halfway through, handed to me and I was told to read aloud to the class. I stumbled over the first paragraph and went red, the whole class tittered or so it felt. I was slowly sinking into the floor.

I went on but managed to mis-pronounce the word 'malfunction', it somehow came out as 'malfluncsion'. I stopped to re-attempt the word and more 'tittering' ensued—the teacher then drove the final nail home by saying:

"*Simon seems to have 'malfunctioned'.* The class erupted into laughter. I don't clearly remember the next bit, but I can still vividly remember the sound of the door slamming as I left the classroom.

I've not, until recently, gone back to reading and I still find it difficult to get any way into a book, I don't think it's due to that experience, I'm just not sure reading is for me. When I do read, I want to analyse every little part of the sentence, the meaning, the feelings, the possibilities. I can hear some people saying 'yes that is what reading is about', but for me it often means reading a paragraph several times and I eventually give up with the book as it is not following what in my mind are the logical steps the story should. I suppose I just don't have that ability like someone such as Taryn does to enjoy the work, let it flow and go with it.

If you've met Taryn, then you'll know that she wasn't going to let that stand as an excuse not to write, so here I am.

So, why am I telling you this? Really just to explain the fact that I then found computers, soon after this happened. The ZX Spectrum was released and I got one for Christmas—this was an eye opener! Remember, this is back in the early 80s and I'd grown up without phones, internet, Xbox, PlayStation, Gameboys etc. The world had just changed forever and now I was moving to a new house with my own room and a ZX Spectrum and a Walkman.

WOW, it was like I was going to be in the film Tron, and I was Jeff Bridges. Games like the EPIC Space Invaders were around—this was the golden age, I had an Atari, Olivetti, BBC Micro the full shebang. Cross those films with the noise that came out of a game as it was loading on the ZX, books just became something else, why would I read after that! I got into the internet at the very beginning and have lived in the matrix ever since, I don't read books, just screens and code. Some would say I have missed a massive opportunity. The point is, are our kids and the current generation more like me? I mean, are they, having been exposed to electronics from a young age, more inclined to watch a screen than read a book? Obviously. There is no question of that.

Google will have us all watching only video in the future if given the chance. It's building more and more knowledge and the AI of what to show someone at the right moment is frightening. Answer Engines are becoming more and more sophisticated to the extent that even Facebook thinks it's a search engine now, listening to every word we say through

WhatsApp etc. Do we give in to being served up mind controlling content? Let's be honest here, nobody is denying that the search engines are exploited by advertisers off the back of the tools and AI available—that's a given. There are bigger things to worry about such as computers becoming sentient and Skynet. But should we really laugh?

All I can say is that YouTube sits there, currently as probably the best and most underutilised opportunity still to market a product. I still learn something every day, most of which is only fascinating in a geeky kinda way and that is why I'm mostly locked away in my bunker, kept away from other humans as much as possible. I encourage anyone who loves data and marketing to get all the Google Skillshop qualifications and experiment with all the possibilities you can create in custom audiences.

Test, test, analyse, rinse and repeat.

## Andy

I got Es in English at school.

I've always struggled with language and the ads I've written have always been in my own style.

But I got around it and think I actually ended up being decent at communicating in a variety of ways. I did an online course for a Uni entrance requirement when I was 40 and got the equivalents to a "c"—so I'd obviously improved. Somehow!

# Writing this book

"Write a book", Simon said. "It will be good for us. It will be great."

To be honest when he said it I thought to myself "you can f**k right off Simon". There is no way on God's earth I can write a book. Not even one with him doing half (probably a fair bit more actually). And not even with the help of the awesome Taryn.

There is no way Andy Price is writing a book.

I'm not a big fan of reading. A book really has to grab me. And I certainly don't like writing loads of words. Hell no.

I just kept thinking...

Not
A
Bloody
Chance.

I'm more likely to go to the moon than to get a book published. And at the point of writing, I still thought it might not happen as Taryn could turn around and say it's a load of old boll*cks.

But here I am.

Writing a book.

About digital wizardry and a bit of ad and brand shizzle.

**Places I have written this book**

When this section was suggested I did have a laugh to myself. So, here it is, the places that I have spent time writing this book:
- Sat in the kitchen
- On the sofa
- Sat on a garden chair in the sun
- At my desk
- Whilst walking talking into my mobile
- Dictating into my mobile whilst travelling (I wasn't driving!)
- Typing into my laptop on my travels to see friends

As a side note here are the places I've had high ideas for the book:
- Waking up in the night
- Whilst having a beer
- Whilst walking
- Whilst cycling
- Whilst cooking
- Whilst driving
- Yes, while being on the toilet haha!
- Whilst being on a boring zoom meeting
- Whilst being on a zoom meeting that wasn't boring
- Cutting the grass and doing the gardening
- Whilst watching TV
- Whilst listening to music

# ▶ The History of YouTube | Simon

▶ The domain name youtube.com was first activated and the site was born effectively on Valentine's Day February 14th, 2005. It took the guys who built it, Jawed Karim, Steve Chen and Chad Hurley, a month before they uploaded the very first video that went on the channel. 'Me at the Zoo', featured them at the San Diego Zoo on April 23rd 2005; and that video can still be seen on the site today.

Obviously, YouTube is now one of the most visited websites on the internet and the three guys who started it had realised back in 2004, that there wasn't one location on the internet where videos could be shared by individuals. They had originally thought of the idea as somewhere that online dating could happen and individuals could upload videos of themselves, but that idea failed. Then they realised that they had managed to create a platform for individuals to put any video up, not just dating profiles. They secured the first round of funding in late 2005, when a seed investor put 3.5 million behind the idea. The investor and partner of the firm that owned PayPal joined the YouTube board in April 2006. By March 2006, the site had more than 25 million videos uploaded and was generating around 20,000 uploads a day.

It was already one of the fastest-growing sites in the world and by the following summer it was delivering an average of 100 million video views a day. But this didn't come without problems. The rapid growth in users meant YouTube had to keep up with the technology. They needed to match the insane numbers of people they were bringing onto the platform on a daily basis. Other problems included copyright infringement and at this point they had not commercialised YouTube.

Google, who had failed at launching their own video platform then looked at them as the best option for growth. In October 2006, it was announced that the company was going to be bought by Google at a valuation of 1.6 billion. The sale went through the month after-—November 2006. At the time this was Google's second biggest acquisition, it was at this point YouTube really kick-started its rise to becoming the global video upload platform that it is today and establishing itself as a multi-billion-dollar business.

It's bigger than TV. It's bigger than any other media markets.

It now funds the lifestyles of hundreds of thousands of YouTubers. Jump forward a year and the founding members of YouTube are each valued at more than 400 million pounds each.

One interesting fact is that it's estimated that in 2007, YouTube consumed as much bandwidth as the entire internet did in 2000. Moving forward, it has hosted presidential debates, film teaser premieres, had many of the world's top brands use it as their primary channel and now hosts many full-length premieres and shows. Looking into 2010, YouTube rebranded and launched a new design which had a simple interface, so that people could spend more time on the platform with ease. It began streaming certain content for free including cricket matches, such as the Indian Premier League.

This was to become commonplace as YouTube started the first worldwide, free, online broadcasting platform for a major sporting event. At this point the site was serving more than 2 billion videos every single day and by May the following year, the site was getting more than 3 billion views a day.

Jump forward to 2012 and we're up to 4 billion views a day. In 2012, YouTube also announced that there were roughly 60 hours of new videos uploaded to the site every single minute, and three-quarters of the material was at this point coming from outside of the USA, with over 800 million unique users a month.

Back in 2010, YouTube was already the third most visited website on the entire internet, after Google and Facebook. One important point to make was that in 2012, YouTube changed its algorithm, moving from a 'view based system', to a 'watch time-based system'. This was credited for causing a surge in the popularity of all the gaming channels on YouTube. In this year, the video 'Gangnam Style' became the first YouTube video ever to surpass 1 billion views and the number of unique visitors early in 2013 surpassed 1 billion in the month of May 2013.

It took until 2013/14 for one of YouTube's own channels to surpass PewDiePie's channel, to become the most subscribed channel on the website. This is mainly down to YouTube suggesting to new users that they subscribe to the channel when they first registered to the site.

YouTube has even allowed a new job title to exist in the whole world, as many aspire to become YouTubers. Initially people didn't just do this for money, it was seen as a hobby and I'm sure, many successful YouTubers who started their channels during the early days, would have never thought that making videos could become a full-time job.

Those channels that are big enough to monetise are able to drive revenue from the ads that appear within the videos uploaded to their channels. Popular YouTubers can earn millions.

Over and above that, many YouTubers are working with sponsors and brands to collaborate and review products, whilst being paid handsomely to do so. Many kids still aspire to be YouTubers today, my own in fact, have their own channels and are avidly looking at the statistics of people watching their videos, how many are subscribing, liking and commenting and such. Whether they'll make it as YouTubers... who knows, but if they manage to apply the same level of enthusiasm to their schoolwork and then their future job prospects, they'll be a massive success!

My 13-year-old son Charlie is an avid fan of VR; and I really do believe virtual reality is going to be one of the bigger video upload styles over the next few years. The only thing holding it back at the moment is the lack of YouTubers really promoting this equipment. That being said, it's lockdown in 2020 and I find myself struggling to purchase a VR set! The experience it brings is amazing and it's bound to lead to a far more immersive experience in the future; perhaps where we could approach a scenario where we build the Oasis, as shown in the film 'Ready Player One'. Who knows where this will end up, your guess is as good as mine, but one thing is for sure, it's not going away.

Obviously, advertising is YouTube's main revenue driver, but the fact that it shares this revenue with its partners (the people uploading videos, the 'YouTubers'), enables people to earn a fortune if their content can go viral, or if they can gain a really high subscriber base. If more people are willing to digest their content, giving them views and engaging with their channels on a daily basis, then this will mean YouTube will gain more users. The cycle then begins. As more channels begin uploading more videos and bringing in higher numbers of users, it leads to more videos being uploaded to the site. This means more videos, more ads and more revenue!

If you go back to 2010, there were roughly fifty hours of video being uploaded to YouTube every minute. Fast forward to 2019, and there's five-hundred to six-hundred hours of video being uploaded to the platform every minute. It won't be long before we reach the thousand hours per minute milestone.

But where will this all end up? Are we going to end up with more content than viewers can consume at some point? Today you have influencers and YouTubers who receive hundreds of thousands, if not millions of subscribers and a lot of these channels are driven by kids watching what I would call, not necessarily nonsense, but certainly content that wouldn't stand up on its own right and would definitely not be viewable on TV. These channels have a high following with fans watching and engaging, but it's also, to some extent, a mind-numbing experience for these kids. Are they learning, who knows? Are they learning things we don't want them too? Probably. Are we teaching them to be something we don't want them to be? Most definitely!

So, there will come a point at which the quality on the platform will need to improve. We are seeing an overwhelming amount of collaboration with channels and brands now and this will definitely increase as we go forwards. This ranges from brands sponsoring channels and giving away products, to getting recommendations and working with influencers. This is all to drive product sales across the platform and Google shopping. Furthermore, we are going to get more in app, or in video purchasing over the next few years. It's already taken off in Japan and other countries, especially on other platforms such as Instagram and TikTok. ∎

# ▶| The Agency Landscape | Simon

▶ The Agency Landscape is broken and has been for a long time, but things are set to change! At the point of writing, during the COVID-19 outbreak, it is expected that 2 out of 5 people within the creative industry in both the UK and USA, will lose their jobs in 2021, due to the after-effects of the virus. What will this mean?

Many new small agencies are set to spring up out of necessity and with a lack of agency positions, more people will be enticed to begin working for themselves. The problem with this, is that they will all be entering a new world, where clients are rare, advertising budgets are going to be spent more carefully (yay) and skilled people will be able to demand a premium.

The worry is loads of 'brand new shiny agencies' spin up, you know the types, the ones who have amazing beards and waistcoats and sell the dream—I'm hoping we can move past that, after all that was pre-COVID, and the new normal will demand something better. It's not to say that there will not be a place for waist-coated and mustachioed hipsters with their swanky offices, beanbags, hammocks and PlayStation 5s. They will never be extinguished! It's just more likely that results will become the name of the game and the 'swish-swash' just won't cut it anymore!

The fundamental problem with the 'agency' model has always been providing transparency of hours worked to the client. Many agencies will charge a base rate of perhaps £50 to £500 an hour, and it's hard to justify to the client when projects have any creep, or the client doesn't have enough clarity of the work that has been undertaken or skill involved. And there it is, the elephant in the room that nobody ever acknowledges—skill, and the value therein.

We, as agency owners, know our worth. We have built our experience, honed our skills, and know 'just where to tap the hammer', but when a client wants results they are coming at it from several angles—why would he or she pay thousands for a few hours work in their eyes? The answer should just be as simple as this—"the guys with the skill will get the results", however, there are SO many agencies out there not producing tangible results, that it inevitably gives a whole swathe of opinion; to the point that so many charge for so little and then everyone is suddenly tarred with the same brush. Ah, but now I hear those with the real skill singing loudly about, "well if you're great at what you do then the best clients come to you", true, very true in fact, but the really successful companies out there are already working with the best. Or are they?

The wider field of 'full service' agencies tend to have some very skilled people and a whole pack of supporting staff. The client wants to work with the skilled person (the organ grinder) and this is where agencies go wrong, in my humble opinion. There is only one of you, but there aren't many clients out there that will pay the thousands per hour to direct the hammer in the right place, in a transparent way. I'm hoping I'm not sounding too bitter at this point, so I'll try and elaborate more about the industry and its future and let's see how far I get. Perhaps I can revisit this and see how wrong I am in 10 years, that being a lifetime in internet terms. We are about to see the largest number of marketing agencies ever, spin up as start-ups, everyone will be clambering for business.

## Those that DO and those that talk

In our game, there are a growing number of agency owners or 'creative homebodies'. 'Creative homebodies' are the people who have had a small level of success with ads and now think they are going to be a world beater, who see the bright lights of earning money while they sleep. Many of these people are what I like to call 'wow merchants' and just like the guys who'd show you a shiny briefcase, you know, like the one in reservoir dogs, or the magic elixir salesman from the wild west, they are the ones claiming to be the go-to 'gurus'.

They put up their seemingly incredulous results from XYZ client who's just achieved 8× ROI with cold traffic and exclaim from the rooftops and in their ads that, "My ads will beat yours, day in day out". What are they selling? Not services, no, they are selling the dream! They are selling the 'this is how you do it', not the 'this is truly what you need to do, and we will hold your hand and guide you along the way.' These people with little knowledge are very dangerous, they don't, as a rule, have any real depth of marketing and advertising knowledge, they don't really care if your campaigns live or fall on their arse, all they want to do is sell you a £47 course, take your money and run for the hills, safe in the knowledge that 90% of their 'students' or 'disciples' will not bother to see the course through in the first place.

Value equals next to nothing. They sit back in their bedrooms, ploughing more and more money into Facebook for the knowledge that every pound they put in, they get two back. Great business for them, for now! Don't get me wrong, there are a whole load of these guys out there, and in comparison a few good ones, but discerning who's any good is a problem, especially when so many business owners have had bad experiences. This is why you need to find a 'doer'. I've always said, if you see someone actively promoting a course for social ads online or especially on Facebook, beware, ask yourself, "Wouldn't these guys be servicing 100s if not thousands of clients and making a fortune, if they were as good as they clearly say they are?"

## Laziness in Advertising, what's gone wrong

It's all too easy to be lazy, poor creatively and to work with no real effort. This is a symptom of how quickly digital advertising has evolved and how relatively easy it has become to drive such levels of success. Google and Facebook in particular have made their tools extremely easy to use, the most famous and easily referenced of those being the Facebook 'Boost' button. I'm sure that 99% of you who are reading this, most likely know about the boost button on Facebook, but for those that don't, it's a tool Facebook introduced to allow pretty much any business with a presence on the platform, to be able to promote their page or content easily. The downfall being that targeting options while using the boost button were massively limited to keep the tool as simplified as possible, what it did lead to though, was mass access to the audiences Facebook had to offer—suddenly anyone was a 'Facebook Ads master'.

Not only did the boost button allow anyone to spend money quickly on Facebook, in the early years, it allowed pretty much anyone who felt like turning their hand to a touch of advertising to achieve reasonable results, with very little effort. Surprisingly, people still use it, although I think this is limited to perhaps smaller one person businesses, promoting into their local areas for example. Most businesses who want results now either use an agency or the more in-depth tools available through Facebook Ads/Business Manager. However, as it is still easy to achieve good results with a modicum of effort, many don't use the deeper audience targeting, remarketing or full use of the AI.

The same applies with Google Ads. Both of the platforms have so many tools available to the advertiser, it takes years to master them all and with more and more functionality being added every month, there are plenty of tools within these platforms that even the most die-hard paid ads aficionados never even touch. I, myself have chatted with Google employees who work in 'ads support' and many a time it is clear, they themselves don't have a clue what I'm talking about, even if it is one of their own tools, then having to make excuses and say they will pass the query to another team and 'get back to you'.

From these early years onwards, Facebook and Google brought to life many so called 'gurus' teaching ads classes and 'secret techniques', of course, everyone had access to all the tools. This meant without any real formal qualifications (aside from the Google Skillshop etc.) that any Tom, Dick or Harry could set themselves up as an agency, running ads for clients and everyone knew more than anyone else.

I do realise the irony of myself and Andy also claiming to be experts. There are tons of great agencies out there, loads of really dedicated people who run excellent, well planned and thought-out campaigns on paid social. But for every one of them, I'd wager there are another 50 'also-rans' or worse, 'charlatans' who claim to be the shizzle when it comes to online advertising, only to fall short on the actual delivery of results, or not having the clients best interest at heart in the first place.

Andy and I wrote and presented an online 'Facebook Ads beginner to master course'. We believe it is one of the very best out there and stand by the fact it gives anyone the opportunity to run ads properly and measure them. We still see next to no agencies running ads which we would consider half decent, for the fact that laziness has become the norm and somehow is acceptable to clients.

As stated before, this springs from the acceptance that anything better than 'just using the boost button' seems to qualify someone as an expert in the field. Whereas in fact, the truth is far from that and even the true experts don't use all the functionality available, unless they are getting paid handsomely to do so. It's become too easy to achieve results, too easy to slap a picture or a video up and choose an audience and achieve some level of success, while blaming any failure on the platform. Clients should be holding their agencies accountable, far more than they currently do. We are, thankfully though, entering a new era where, unless you work with the AI, and many of the tools, plus build an end-to-end funnel and strategy, it is becoming extremely difficult to produce decent results. It's almost as if Facebook, Google etc. planned it all that way by getting everyone addicted and bought in. Now nobody can let go.

As an example (a very simple one), we saw a client who wanted to advertise a 'Time and Attendance System', it was essentially a clocking in system for workers, a nice piece of kit but in a very competitive market. Simply checking all the adverts out there on PPC, showed that as per the Google suggested rules, it was best to include 'Time and Attendance' in the advert headline. Okay, fair enough, those are the words that people are searching for, so it makes sense right? But the lazy advertiser or agency simply spun up ads with 'Looking for the best Time and Attendance system' etc. BORING! Looking at all the ads out there, they ALL had that phrase in there, how could we stand out? How could we help the client be different? How could we pull on the emotions of the person, the potential client that had typed in and had intent to buy a new 'Time and attendance system'?

Easy—we wrote a series of adverts with headlines like 'Oh dear, Sarah is late for work again!' It wasn't rocket science, but it upped the click through by more than 50% and onsite enquiries doubled, which meant Google gave precedence to our ads and the client not only had better results, but saved money in the process. I had to admit to Andy that in the past this would have been beyond me (as I'm the techie side of the business), but having worked with Andy and his creativity, this just made sense to test and the results spoke for themselves.

Not lazy, just creative. But clients do pay for creativity, it's easy isn't it? LOL, two seconds worth of thought saved a client thousands of pounds, but 30 years of experience went into that 2 second thought. So, maybe it is unfair to criticise those without that level of experience and call them lazy. They are not lazy, they have just been brought up in an environment that has so easily yielded success, with all the tools out there, ready and easy to use. They've had no need to look past the horizon.

Yes, there will always be the lazy agency or someone who 'knows a bit about how it works' but it's going to shift. Standout quality creatives, plus execution through the usage of all the tools available will give those advertisers who do it properly a distinct advantage.

## Is Facebook dead and saturated with Ads, what & where next for FB?

Wondering what actually goes on in the life of people like Mark Zuckerberg? I'm of a mind to propose a reality where 'the Zuk', as he shall henceforth be referred to, is sat there in his ivory tower stroking his VR cat and musing over how next he can buy half the earth's land or become richer than Elon, Jeff or Bill. Or even manipulate voters to bring about world peace.

Oh dear, now I have a vision of him dressed in a bikini on stage giving a speech as a pageant contestant. Well, maybe that's not so much of a stretch of imagination and what we get up to in our private lives that's up to us, that's right isn't it Zukky?

Come on though, what on earth must a day in his shoes actually be like? Constant emails to appear at senate hearings, walking into a room where people quickly fall into line, or just visits to his private bowling alley where the pins carry the images of Jeff Bezos and Bill Gates. Or is it daily karaoke parties where he merrily chortles out the entirety of the back catalogue of Coldplay (seriously does nobody realise that Chris Martin is actually the human version of Mark Zuckerberg?).

At least he's not manipulating the cryptocurrency markets like good old Uncle Elon. Talking about Dogecoin as the future currency of Earth and us all becoming a 'multiplanetary species' because he made a game up when he was 12 and now wants that to become all our futures, well not yet at least.

Plenty of time to actually go fully bonkers like Elon Musk. Now that guy is a genius, does anyone want him running their social media platform though? Cue end of the world, where we are all cryogenically frozen until such time we can all move to Mars. In reality Zuk might be just sitting writing a book like me as the sun comes up, who knows, I digress.

He's obviously way past caring about money, so why doesn't he start caring about what's on Facebook a lot more? Perhaps he's fallen out of love with it and he's got plenty of people that now take responsibility for that. The platform as a whole doesn't seem to have developed very much or brought out many new features. Yes, on the advertising front, it's becoming more and more sophisticated, but personally I think that the front end should innovate. Not in terms of changing the interface as that does a perfect job, but the control over the content—now there's the kicker.

They have the tech to remove anything that's racist, offensive, controversial or that mentions certain words. But they don't as Facebook would die.

Yes, people get banned but it relies on the community to be self-policing, it has no option. Sitting above everything on the platform to make sure it grows and lives is engagement, supported by viral content, and in the main without differences of opinion it would fall flat. Facebook is already seen as the domain of an older demographic, yes it has been around longer. Even its younger sister Instagram is faced with that future as other upstarts like TikTok begin to dominate, demonstrating a slow decline in both platforms' growth and eventual demise.

As I write we've just gone through iOS14 and that's causing advertisers on the platform a myriad of problems. As tracking conversions is changing fast, the battle with Apple and others for control of the future of advertising, will be enormously interesting to see play out. The new privacy laws are at the top of the agenda. Maybe there is even a post-it note on Zuks laptop (wonder if it's a Mac?) covering up his webcam that says PRIVACY on it.

The point being, none of us know how privacy is going to affect the internet for advertisers. Google is leading the way with new 'Federated Learning Cohorts', which sounds like a fancy name for *'another way we are going to round you up and get as much information as possible'.*

Remember though, the control sits with the audience, at some point there will be a backlash against privacy infringement. Personally, I can't stand the fact that WhatsApp is listening to my every word yet it's still on my phone. Oooh the conundrum that brings up. Well the toaster and fridge are listening too so it's already way past the point we can do anything about it.

The debate should move to AI very soon and if you haven't watched the YouTube videos of that robot saying 'kill all humans', you should. The robots are coming and as a species we are already redundant living in the Matrix. Mark, Elon, Jeff, what say you?

Andy describes me often in client meetings as 'like Neo from the Matrix', to demonstrate the way I think about numbers and build audiences for Google campaigns. My worry is that many marketers forget that you can build your own audiences within Google, taking the easy way out and using the off-the-shelf audiences. Over and above that we are already in a scenario where we've been suckered into a world where Google, Facebook and the other advertising platforms completely control everything.

It may sound like I'm Facebook bashing, well I am a little. Having seen the tools in depth on both Facebook and Google it's very easy for me to draw the conclusion that Google leads the way. Can Facebook pivot and change its ways?

I've talked about it a lot in the past and it's still enormously important for businesses to take an omni-channel approach to their marketing. Building a funnel that is well thought-out and designed before you get going is essential to success. Still too many times we see clients come to us from other agencies saying that they've *"had someone doing their Facebook"* or *"yes we do Google Search but nothing on YouTube"*.

The way to win is to use all the tools, advertise by collecting the data properly from your conversion events and pass all that data back and forth across Facebook, Google, Instagram, Twitter, YouTube, LinkedIn etc. Doing this whilst ensuring you are hitting your target markets right at the very moment they are ready to buy—not just hoping for a sale on moment one. Learning, testing, reiterating and teaching the algorithms—they are here to stay and a hell of a lot more clever people than us are running the whole shebang. Challenge me if you think otherwise. So, you can either use their tools properly or go throwing darts (and money) and hoping to strike it lucky with the 'silver bullet' campaigns, you know, the ones that just don't seem to work.

Use the tools and the robots they have built for us, but use your intelligence to be better.

**What's that WhatsApp**

Following on from the Facebook point in the previous section, I wanted to ask you to think about WhatsApp, what's that all about? It's free right? Where is the revenue? How can it be valued at billions of dollars? Yes, it has millions upon millions of active users all over the world, but what's the point? WhatsApp provides free communication, 'end-to-end encrypted' really? What is the end-game for it? What plans does Facebook have for WhatsApp, or is it just there to collect marketing information, listening to your communications, analysing the messaging you are sending, looking at the photos you are sending? Worse?

Facebook and Apple are having a nightmare at the moment, with iOS14 and the soon to be iOS15 there is the opportunity for users to block all tracking (the entire marketing industry stood back with mouths wide open and said 'What?!') so that means no conversion events are trackable, how do we then teach campaigns? This is probably the hottest topic in the marketing industry right now, especially if you are a Facebook focused agency. Maybe I should just be saying "get yourselves straight on over to good old YouTube". Oh, hang on a minute the kind people at Apple don't really want you being tracked over there either; aluminum helmets at the ready people, an apple might fall out of the sky, hit you on the head with the word 'conversion' on the side of it. I'm certain William Tell never used WhatsApp while shooting an apple off his son's head and starting a massive revolution. Maybe the secret code name the upper echelons of Apple have for this 'wolf in sheep's clothing' update they call iOS15 is the 'William Tell project', who knows. Maybe we need a super-grass to let us know the real agenda. Maybe we see where Apple aims their next crossbow bolt, any guesses?

Yes there are things that Facebook wants you to do, such as verify your domain, measure conversions over a shorter period etc. There are some fantastic systems out there like Hyros which is pretty revolutionary by allowing ads to scale and feed data back more easily into the campaigns in Facebook and Google. Another we've used, called Wicked, that does the job of getting around the problem by tagging server side rather than keeping a cookie alive. Neither are cheap, but if you are scaling properly then these offer an off-the-shelf supported solution and Hyros has a particularly good community around it, saving a large chunk of time and ads budget.

As the guys at Facebook, Apple and Google battle out the whole privacy and cookie plus attribution conundrum there are going to be lessons learned and challenges to overcome. My advice is to lean heavily on your internal resources putting the right systems and reporting in place, plugging in the data you have from sales, so that you have your own single version of the truth showing where your valuable conversions are coming from. To take it to that next level, you don't just want the conversion data you want the quality of that conversion and to tie that back into your marketing efforts. Plug in your CRM and feed that data back to your campaign managers and you'll see exponential growth, so few people we meet do this and it frankly beggars belief. As always the more data you have the more you can optimise and as privacy becomes more and more an issue we may well see the sizes of lookalike and custom audiences shrinking or their effectiveness waning. This is when it is going to become super important to have all the right systems in place. I've talked a great deal about putting in place thoroughly thought out and planned omni-channel remarketing loops, this is where the big wins will be seen by those of you who have the full funnel mapped out and a clear strategy to mop up everything on the back end, tie back that valuable conversion types as well and you'll beat 95% of your competition plus probably save half your budget in the process. Traffic isn't going to be an issue, designing those audiences will be a massively skilled job and the challenges for attribution of conversion will only demand a more intricate solution. So is WhatsApp a problem, well not for Facebook. Apple on the other hand, maybe they think there's a real problem there. I'll leave you to draw your own conclusions, it will be fascinating to see how it all plays out over the next few years.

## Reach Various Audiences on different platforms & devices

You can now use highly targeted campaigns by device or platform, which creates some amazing opportunities. As a basic example, we could choose to target only people who are using iPhone X or above (device targeting), surfing YouTube between 7pm and 10pm (timed), who are female 45+ (demographics), living in Manchester (location), have searched for "Yves Saint Laurent" (Keywords), been In-market for beauty products (Topics) and so forth. Taking this even further we can even target people who have been on specific apps or competitor's websites, watching particular channels and videos on YouTube and then layer several of these together (layering is the trick to real success with YouTube ads).

- ▶ topics
- ▶ placements
- ▶ audiences
- ▶ times
- ▶ demographics
- ▶ keywords

Targeting where these intersect for the optimised opportunity to create a conversion (i.e. Not just relying on one audience source).

Audiences are constantly moving away from TV, that is a fact. People are shifting onto the various digital platforms and using them more and more as part of their daily lives. Brands therefore need to find ways to cut through all the digital noise and compete. As times change more and more brands will come onto YouTube, we will see some brands using their TV ads on YouTube (this can be a mistake though), which some are already. YouTube still offers them an enormous opportunity. I myself, have very occasionally been accused of being a 'Facebook basher', in that, I have moaned about the ever changing and movable feast that is Facebook and its ads. Currently as I write, my personal opinion is that Facebook is trying hard to up its game, wanting to charge more for advertising space (some days my feed is completely saturated and others next to nothing, so they are testing continually). But does Facebook have the same ability as Google for targeting?—I think not.

## Overcharging—The 'pay per lead' model

I've always found some of the business models that some agencies use to be distasteful—that being a 'pay per lead' charging structure. The main reason being that there is a complete lack of transparency. Having generated many thousands of leads myself over the years, for financial services companies in particular, it has become apparent on occasion that some of the clients my agency was generating leads for, went on to then broker these leads to several other customers at a significant markup—not okay in my opinion.

Take a scenario where we have generated a lead for a young couple, who are looking for a mortgage on their first home.

That lead may have cost £5 or £10 to produce once you take into account advertising spend, agency fee, website landing page build, social media posting, blogging, videos, creative time and such. Okay, you only reach this cost per lead once you've got a well-oiled machine and a funnel that is working well, alongside a trusted site. But take that lead, give it to an unscrupulous company who came to you under the pretext of being a mortgage broker wanting the leads for themselves, then find out they are reselling those same leads to others. Not great, especially when you find they are selling the same lead 3 or 4 times at an average of £40-£60 a go! And sometimes even higher.

Now, some may say, well done, they have a business model that is working for them. Having employed our agency to produce them at under £10, they are simply selling on what they rightfully paid for. The lead is therefore a tradable commodity. NO, that young couple didn't sign up to get 4 or more phone calls, have their details shared to third parties who they have no agreement with. This is just one example of where the pay per lead model gets abused. Take it one step further and you might imagine a scenario where I, as the lead generator, then go on to demand 'my share of the profits' from the person or business I'm selling the leads to—again NO. There will be some of you reading this perhaps who have a business that operates exactly in this way, shame on you, your time will come.

As an agency we have a duty to be transparent about the work we do and the charges we make for that work. That doesn't include taking a slice out of the client's business or potentially holding them to ransom (i.e. switching off their leads, switching off their business).

So, now that you understand some of my thinking behind my hatred of the 'pay per lead' model, let's apply that scenario to the social media networks and big online marketplaces. As things are progressing, it is not hard to imagine a scenario where these tech giants effectively OWN your business, and by that I mean, you are so reliant on the orders that come through a particular channel, that without them you would fail. You have become so completely dependent on their 'shelf space' or 'advertising slots' that they 'own you'. Scary isn't it? Many clients of mine in the past have been highly reliant on their leads from Facebook and Google, uncomfortably so sometimes.

Amazon is a prime example here. See what I did there? A 'prime' example, anyway it made me chuckle briefly. They have been accused many times of sucking in sellers, letting them build big businesses, then suddenly the advertiser finds that the rules have changed, or the ground has shifted.

The unsuspecting advertiser with their nice profitable business, then sees Amazon bringing in their own 'Amazon recommends' products at a cheaper price. Then said advertiser who was previously running a profitable business now has their listings in a less favourable position. Overnight their business is crushed, through literally no fault of their own. Who do you think the factory in China wants to deal with, Mr or Mrs X, who runs a business in the UK and buys sporadically, or Mr Bezos who guarantees millions of dollars a month to them? Mr Bezos will then likely go on to purchase the factory, does that mean we should all shut up shop now and await the world (I'm imagining a scene from Blade Runner or Robocop now) where anything we want is delivered literally seconds from requesting it, after we have paid out our hard-earned credits (don't get me started on DeFi and crypto we could have another whole book on our hands). This is just an extension of and a weird imaginary version of the 'pay per lead' model, but by this point all agencies, shops, resellers, distributors etc. are all long-gone and everything is supplied direct from the source. Sounds grim doesn't it?

Now pause and take a look at Facebook and Google—both want your advertising revenue, both operate a model where the more you pay, the higher your listings. Neither yet has ventured into the supply business by trying to turn themselves into a product manufacturer/seller. It's clearly not their plan. They are solidly focused on being the advertising space, the influencer of decisions, the conduit through which most eCommerce trade and new business is generated. Their not so hidden agenda is to take a bigger and bigger cut of the profits and tie you into the fact you must pay to survive.

Many industries simply cannot use Google/Facebook etc. purely because the margin in their product doesn't support the listings, let alone the advertising spend. Compare them to LinkedIn—Microsoft's shiny B2B platform where to advertise you might pay somewhere in the region of £20—£40 for a thousand impressions. Facebook, in comparison, is somewhere currently at around £5 for a thousand. LinkedIn has the luxury of being B2B and therefore demanding a premium. They also took the decision, a long time ago, to actively discourage the smaller businesses from advertising on their platform. By stopping low quality adverts, it means that the newsfeed on LinkedIn isn't flooded with ads of a similar quality to those on Facebook. There is only one way this is all going. Costs to advertise are continually creeping up, space is at a premium, we've seen many Facebook ads accounts getting suspended or banned for no apparent reason recently. YouTube doesn't suffer from a lack of space.

Yes, it's an auction and a competition for space. The networks want us, as advertisers, to pay more and to be better creatively. It will become the survival of the fittest. Over the next few years we will see those with the bigger budgets winning out, and smaller advertisers getting squeezed out. It's literally turning into an online advertising war and we are not in control. Where will it all end up? One thing is for sure though, those with the best adverts (and by that I mean creative and engagement) will outlive the average, creative will actually be king in the end.

Your guess is as good as mine at this point. I don't like the idea that in the future there will be only 3 or 4 companies controlling the global economy, but it could happen. I hope not, but it could, couldn't it? Maybe we all join the 'aluminium helmet brigade', pushing back as a society, against being ushered into a future where we are all handing 30% or more of our businesses to them, just to get a seat at the table.

Google is currently creating much debate within its own Google Partner programme. As someone who has held an MCC ('My Client Centre'), the type of Google manager account where agencies control the ads for their clients, for 20 years, I'm concerned, and so are many thousands of my peers all across the globe. Google has always made 'recommendations', the ones that pop up to supposedly help the advertisers as friendly suggestions, in reality these recommendations are really there to 'help you spend more money'.

The recommendations Google makes have always needed to be taken with a pinch of salt—some are good, but some can be misleading. However, Google is now threatening to change the rules, and currently 'hinting' heavily that if its partner agencies 'don't follow at least a very large number of these recommendations' then they can have their partner status revoked. The agency community is, in some respects, rebelling against this. Many don't care as they want full control of the client's accounts, but it is becoming more and more necessary to implement recommendations or suffer poor campaign performance. We are being boxed in. Could this be a precursor to Google automating the whole thing and taking out the agency world? Not yet, but it is not hard to imagine a scenario where they effectively force agencies to toe the line at some point in the future. Conspiracy theories are not hard to justify at this point. Recently I've seen Google rinsing certain accounts, this is worrying as well as seeing costs go up only indicates one thing (well I can't see them going back down)—Google is testing how much it can squeeze out of advertisers all the time.

Getting back to 'pay per lead', we are all paying for space, yes, but are we willing to give up a chunk of our businesses? I don't think we have a choice as it stands. All the big tech and social marketing companies are cornering the market, only societal change will break that pattern. Legislation is toothless. All this paints a very bleak picture. The lesson to learn though is, don't put all your eggs in one basket—use a multi-channel approach to your advertising. I've seen so many businesses taken out in 24 hours by seeing their one channel fall off a cliff, so make sure when you are approaching your ads not to rely too heavily on one of the networks in isolation.

## Overcharging—The retainer model

This section (from my perspective) isn't just about retainers, but the whole way the industry bills for its services. It's also about how clients view the payment of these services.

**Rant alert. Rant alert.**

There are so many different types of agencies. Ad agencies, design companies, brand development companies, internal communication agencies, media agencies, PPC agencies, social agencies, SEO agencies, through the line agencies, direct marketing agencies, shit agencies, really amazing agencies, okay-ish agencies, one-man bands, and last of all global giants.

I guess it's the same from the client side. Small, big, lots of shapes and sizes.

Some massive agencies work on the big fat retainer model and they need to because they probably have 100's if not 1000's of staff when managing multiple global accounts. There needs to be contracts and re-assurance both ways for a period of time. Indeed, it doesn't matter what size you are, both parties need reassurance. That's where the retainer model can be tricky. How long it runs for, get out clauses, deliverables, over delivering from an agency perspective and not being remunerated sufficiently as you are tied into a fee. There can be times where the client isn't really getting value either. Yes, there are all kinds of clauses and paybacks. But it can be so complicated, and the relationship becomes transactional rather than relationship based. One where trust, debate, understanding, fairness and transparency are core rather than the dollars.

I'm not saying they don't work. It's just that it's hard work.

But the same goes for pay as you go. It's a constant race to the bottom in my view, particularly with public tender stuff (and don't get me started on jobs for the boys).

Cheap, fast and fleece is how I view them.

Again, not relationship based.

Then there are performance related payments. Or at least part of the fee is.

I've never seen one work well myself. In my honest opinion of why, it's because the expectations are always unrealistic and fundamentally, they don't take into account unforeseen circumstances. Look at COVID!!!!

I'm not going to keep going on here because quite frankly, it bores me.

When you sit down and debate like fair grown ups you can find ways and a good common ground to begin working from. You work hard, you deliver the results, you enjoy yourself and the client is happy. They haven't been ripped off. Neither have we. Everyone wins. It's not about it being cheap. It's not about it being expensive.

At the end of the day it comes down to one word.

Value.

Value each other, value what you give. Value what you want to receive.

## Where the future of ads lie

If you haven't seen 'Minority Report', a Tom Cruise film set in the future (2054) in Washington D.C., then have a watch. If you have, then you may be able to remember a scene where he's walking through a lobby in an airport and the walls are completely covered in video screens, the ads change as he is walking past them and are all tailored exactly to him. We are seeing this happen already to an extent and it has to be the future. Maybe Google knows what you want before you know what you want. Your toaster can tell what mood you are in by how hard you push the button and the conversations you're having in the kitchen. Wait, no, it's the future, there is no button and the toaster has gone on strike as you've shown favoritism to the fridge and they are now having a tiff.

Let's go back to 2014, we were working with a large multi-site holiday business based in the UK (give it a go at guessing, there are only a handful, and this is the biggest one). They came to us wanting to increase sales in their bars, that being the main profit centre for when customers were on site. Discussions eventually led to getting people out of their rooms as early as possible in the evening. Punters would traditionally bring their own alcohol to the site and sit in their rooms getting suitably lubricated, prior to heading out for the evening into the onsite bars, restaurants and entertainment venues, silent discos and slots. The issue being that for every hour that the bars were full, the business made a lot of money (we will have to leave that as an undisclosed figure, but I can tell you it was A LOT). Not enough bar time hours were being filled as far as the venue was concerned.

So, getting people into the venues earlier, giving them a better 'at bar' experience and serving them more quickly was the brief.

The most challenging part was getting people out of their rooms, this is the behaviour of the typical customer and it had to be changed fundamentally which meant putting on more events (which incurred more cost and was a risky strategy). Initially we were challenged to improve the experience, helping people enjoy their break—the Minority Report scene came into my head whilst I was walking around the venue, with the then Marketing Director, because it was so clear to me that this was a visual experience.

There were hundreds of TVs, screens and the backs of all the bars were covered with them. When the venues were full it was almost impossible to hear over the music and the only choice (the better one) was to visually engage the audience/customers. How could we improve this? With personalisation of course, imagine a scenario where you walk up to the bar and the drinks are ready for you, or the screens change to influence your purchase by displaying the brand you were most disposed to.

Take it further and think about offers and promotions in which bar staff engage with the video and encourage the punters to try or buy drinks that the venue would either make more profit margin on or gain sponsorship from. The drinks brands and video content were not the problem, the issue was the audience, as there could be 100s of people looking at or standing near to the bar at any one time.

This is where NFC came in, could we pull data about the crowd in general? Could we identify individuals and their likes and dislikes? Pretty much all of the customers were carrying mobile phones with their social media on them logged in. What was the general age group in front of the bar, was it primarily male or female etc.? Lots of possibilities. Could we track and map the movement of guests? Could we get the bartender to say "*Hello XXXX how are you, your usual*?", knowing that the person who approached the bar had purchased X before. Could we even analyse the purchases by age, gender, family unit and learn what to serve or suggest next? Could we serve content that actively moved people from one venue to the next (something we worked on with other pub chains). Maybe, and yes we did achieve this in some cases.

So, where am I going with this? The point being is that we could tell people a story, exactly what they wanted to see and when we could anticipate their actions. We could manipulate their decisions and make them do what we wanted. We could keep them in venues longer and make them spend more and when they were ready to leave, we actively moved them to another offer in another venue on site. If there was an uplift in spend per customer per visit, could we post ads for the events 'just at the right time' to social media and then get them to engage with the posts on Facebook at the time? We needed them to be facilitating, engaging and therefore sharing viral ads to similar audiences (their friends and people like them). It was like magic. It's only a fraction of what is possible with digital social influence.

YouTube offers similar opportunities, not only does it allow videos to come up for very competitive search terms at the top of Google within days of being published, it also allows us to set sequences, not that many agencies even know this feature exists, or they are too lazy to bother to set up the 'if this then that' sequences of videos. One of the most successful tactics you can use with InStream Ads is 'If someone watches video one, then show them video two, if they then skip video two show them video four, if they watch video two show them three', etc. Hopefully you can see how powerful that could be. ∎

# ▶ Social Media | Simon

▶ When did we forget it is called *'Social Media'*?

The clue is in the words. I've spoken about this for a long time, SOCIAL media, not SALES media. Let's look back to when social started, every company seemingly jumped on and said, "We need a Facebook page, a Twitter profile, now, who can we get to do that?"

Typically, the directors in charge of businesses at this point were in their 30's and 40's, even older, the point being none of them understood the potential of social media, nor did they think it would last or be a real tool for business to drive engagement and new leads. Whoops. What happened next still has massive ramifications. Those directors looked around their company, looked for someone who was young, perhaps someone who was just out of university. Let's call our example 'Sarah', she's 21, so she's young and therefore, she must understand this new *'social media thingy'*—let's give her the job of doing that Facebook and Twitter (it's not going to be that important).

Oh, dear me, we forgot, that poor young Sarah might not have any formal training or qualifications in marketing, if any qualifications or experience at all, this social media thing is new, she can learn it. As a side note, working in the marketing industry, I see very few people that actually understand marketing. Many 'do' it or are competent, few are imaginative and combine that with actual marketing. Anyway, back to Sarah's story, she's got the job! Yay, she's now got to think about what she's going to do, what's she going to post, how can that turn into a benefit for the business?

Sarah has little or no marketing experience, her cat probably has more, bearing in mind that at this time in history, millions of people are just getting into using social media. So what does she post? INFORMATION about the company? She's written blogs, right?

Sales literature, maybe a blog (oooh), pictures of the team, perhaps some upcoming events, but it is all about the business and nothing to do with personality or the people behind the business! It's not her fault, what was she supposed to do? Nobody else in the business is probably helping, or knows how to help, the people that matter don't get it (which is still very true today to a large extent) and social media is in lots of older people's minds, a 'necessary evil' or something they 'just don't do or get involved with'. Are you starting to see the problem? Sarah's boss hasn't ever seen their Facebook page, but knows they have one, good enough.

Sarah is left alone and out of the social activity is coming SALES—after all that is the end result we want right? We want more sales and more customers but how do we do that? We post about products and benefits; we post flyers, pictures, maybe some promotions, but Sarah at this point is not creating a conversation. Note the word 'conversation', something that is dying out in society now, and social media has a lot to do with it because 'social media' became 'sales media' and it happened overnight. Swipe right, short attention, little engagement, oh well.

There are still a very large number of 'Sarah's' out there, social media managers thinking that posting is about sales. My God, even some of the people working for me don't get it, there are STILL sales posts going out on my own company's social media as I write this, it drives me bananas. It doesn't take much creative thought to get away from this attitude, but the default is always to go back to sales—please NO! Social media should be used for conversation, debate, personality, education, engagement and sharing knowledge. Sales then comes off the back of this, and I hate the way people use the word 'authentic' as that's what we all need to be on social media, but who's really doing that? Only a few people and very few brands (who then get the sack for not posting the right content). The challenge being to get past the corporate handcuffs and grey suits who placed the initial rules on content, those people in charge of companies that just don't get it.

They will never get it and I've given up wasting my breath trying to educate and enthuse them as to any reason why they should. They don't understand and wrote off social media long ago. It could take a couple of generations to fix the problem (let's hope lots of the Sarah's went and got marketing qualifications). I see it all the time, ask a client to be brave and out there on social media, to appoint social media ambassadors, reward their teams for engagement and sales generated. Eyeballs roll, or there is an admission and again, it's gone over the person's head.

Then the teams have great ideas for content and campaigns and at the point the content plan is to be signed off. It is watered down at the frustration of the agency or the creative team that expended so much effort, and then it falls flat. I'm always preaching to brands about their content feeling a bit stale, or saying that what you are putting out is equivalent to that noise that Charlie Brown's mother made 'Bahh Bahh Bee Bah Bah' or something like that. It doesn't matter exactly what it sounded like as it was indiscernible and nobody was listening. It's a bit like the majority of brands on social media. They're boring, sales like and post nondescript content for the sake of content sake—please stop wasting your time if that sounds like your brand. Anyways, you can't teach an old dog new tricks, so where does that leave the industry? If you don't change your ways it's only going to get harder with video marketing, hard enough to think what to make and post about 'sales'. Heaven help these dinosaurs if they want to make video!

Get ready for a whole new bunch of sales media. Yes, there are lots more people doing it right (or at least trying to), those are the guys and girls I love, but they are getting weighed down by client constraint and mediocrity. One of the other parts of YouTube that I'm going to talk about quite a lot during this book will be retention and you will simply not retain viewers on your channel unless your content is engaging enough or, 'on topic' enough, so specifying your audience and getting your messaging right with an engaging piece of content is what will win. There are a ton of agencies out there producing video content and pushing it out on YouTube but forgetting the fact that you have to target the audience correctly, and with the right piece of content, at the right time.

There's nothing worse than putting out average content for the sake of it! If your only intention when posting content is to post content then you really shouldn't bother—it's a waste of time.

We are seeing a massive amount of stand-out content now, and this is the next wave of absurdity, catering for an audience. This is an audience that wants the mad, showbiz style, X-factor, personality driven approach. This type of content is hard to control and often impromptu, not consistent and not aligned to an actual campaign objective.

Imagine yourself walking into a pub full of people and shouting out 'Blah Blah Bee Blah Blah'. You're going to grab a lot of attention, some people will get angry, some will just ignore you as you are rugby tackled to the floor. Frankly you are the only person who can and should care.

Most will think you're the local idiot, maybe a couple of people will come and talk to you. Some see this then as success and this 'shock tactic' at least stands out and does drive some sort of result, fancy trying it?

I thought not.

## Addicted to Social Media?

Yes, the world has an addiction and it is only getting worse, so, what's the problem?

People are now actively looking for their daily 'likes', think about it, we are all posting and looking for interactions (note there is no 'dislike' button on Facebook or most of the platforms). Many people are growing up with a mental illness based on the back of social media. I witnessed one of my members of staff in her early 20's having a breakdown, bursting into tears as she'd not received any likes on a post about a new haircut in the first 30 minutes—is this where we want to go as a society?

Another young person I know got lost near London King's Cross Station and was struggling. Rather than walking up to someone and starting a conversation asking for help (which seemed in his mind impossible) he was frantically texting friends at 11pm and not getting answers. He got no reply and went on to post the entire dilemma on Facebook, as if it was going to help (maybe it was a cry for help). This is not the fault of young people, they've grown up with devices in their hands pretty much constantly, continually affirming their lives and it's become an addiction.

Some of my favourite comments on the subject come from Simon Sinek. If you've not seen his work and particularly the interviews about 'snowflakes' then I'd encourage you to have a search on YouTube and watch. The trouble for me is that this is spreading—older generations are finding that they are also becoming addicted, sitting on the sofa scrolling through feeds, sitting in restaurants across from each other not talking, but scrolling, clicking, posting and liking. What the hell is wrong with some of these people? Are their lives so empty that social media has become their only escape?

By now, some of you reading this are saying '*hang on, didn't this guy write some of the best Ads courses for Facebook, isn't he purporting to be the go-to guy for YouTube Ads?'* Well, yes, I'm guilty as charged, is this going to go away?

Well, errr, obviously not, I just like to rant occasionally when I see a young family for example, both parents on their phones (not talking) and their kids either on tablets themselves, or running riot, unchallenged and missing out on the attention they deserve from their parents. Maybe there is no hope?

Maybe we are all going to end up in the IOT or the matrix? It will be very interesting to see how the psychological effects of this addiction play out over the next couple of decades. Your guess is as good as mine, but as I write the prevalence of VR is increasing, will we all be having dinner with our virtual friends at a virtual dinner table, with virtual food in the not so distant future? Grim isn't it?

Personally, I've gone through it all, got bored and seen now where time is better spent. If you think about it and you think perhaps you have a problem with social media, then try staying off your devices for a few days. That will be the test to see if you are truly addicted. Do you even care if you are addicted?

Why am I writing such a long rant about social media when I'm a clear advocate of it?

It's because, when used correctly it is amazing, there is no getting away from it, but what worries me is the use of tracking, profiling and the invasion of privacy; couple that with an ability to spread fake news, and not even fake news—the issue there is a societal one. Where are we going as a society when institutions or brands use social media to influence your life? Influence your everyday life, your decisions, what you buy, how you buy, who you are friends with, what your political beliefs are and more. There seems to be very little control, especially from Facebook. Given the chance Facebook would profile every single last hair on your head and thought in your brain, they would know what you wanted before you wanted it, in fact they would have planted the seed of 'want' there before you even thought of buying that new shiny product.

I was explaining this to several of our young people around the time of the recent election. None of them at the start of the conversation thought they had been influenced by social media posting at all, but once we brought up some examples and showed two girls, of a similar age that they had been targeted by separate parties for different reasons and both had gone on to vote the way they had, both admitted they had indeed been externally influenced (I can hear some people now shouting, that's advertising my friend), but is it fair?

Should it be regulated? Should anyone be allowed to post anything they like, promote it, promote deep fakes, promote stories they know to be false with a hidden agenda and not just to sell products.

I believe there is a big wakeup call coming soon to the social media giants. ∎

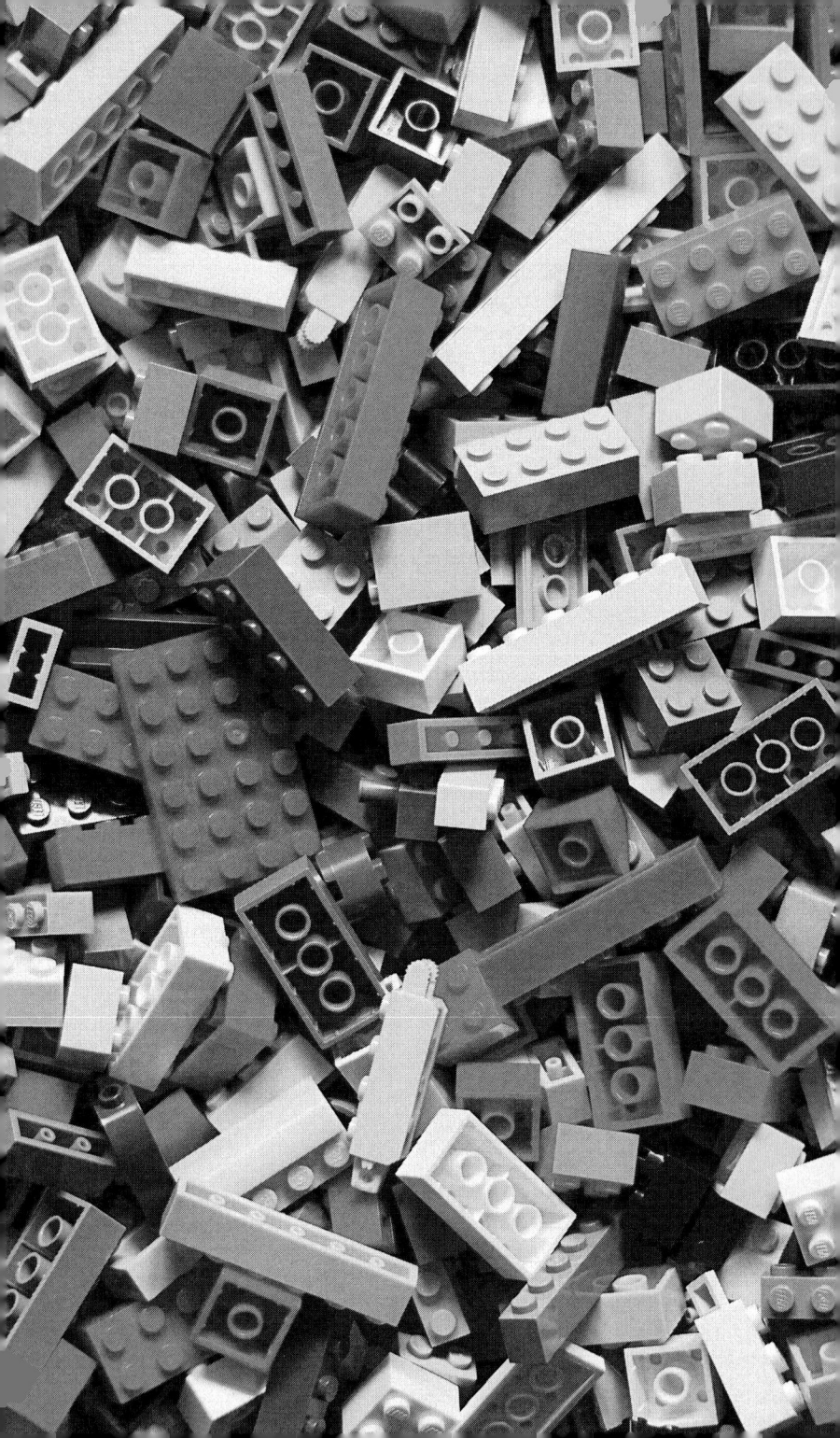

# ⏭ Building a brand | Andy

▶ A note about why I ramble about stuff, that doesn't seem relevant to the future of advertising and YouTube but actually is!

The advertising game is an old one.

There are thousands of books, some bad, some genius. There are thousands, if not millions of website articles and God knows what else in existence as well.

So, you have a lot to go at! You may even think this book is a pile of codswallop.

There are a myriad of opinions. There is a universe full of systems, ways, techniques, tricks and so on that help us to deliver more engaging, interesting ads and ultimately great results for our clients.

The world we live in has changed and the way we consume information has certainly transformed. Mainly technology and how we see, hear, and view things; and this has altered our industry.

But the end game hasn't changed.

Ultimately everyone in our sector is a salesperson. We are helping sell our client's products and services.

And before you pipe up and go *"It's not about selling, it's about sharing stories and engaging with consumers blah blah blah"*.

Yep I get it. New tricks.

But at the end of the day, we are here to help a client sell more. And because of that there are some universal truths that remain the same.

Strong businesses have clear missions, visions and more importantly values. These allow for a strong and clear personality for the brand. One that reflects its customer's needs. And their relationship at its core, has a shared truth, DNA. Once this shit is sorted you can start to communicate things.

If it's not, well, what are you selling?

So, I touch upon what I regard as some fundamental areas. Regardless of whether you were selling soap in 1880, a webinar in 2021, or a flying car in 2089, the way the message gets to the consumer may be different, but the principles will be the same.

Let me start by saying you need a strong brand to utilise any marketing channel, not just with YouTube. So, before I rabbit on about brands on YouTube, maybe I need to talk about what a brand is?

## First, what is a brand?

This is a topic with thousands of articles and many books, written by people much better qualified than I. Having said that I have spent 30 years seeing multitudes of businesses make a complete balls-up of it.

Why? Simple, because they don't believe in it or don't understand it. Or should I say they don't believe in the value of it.

Let me say this once and once only.

Having a strong brand is the most powerful thing any business, anywhere in the world, can embrace to deliver long-term business success.

Fact.

So, what is a brand? How does something so esoteric work in a cut-throat business world?

Let's start by saying what it is not.
- ▶ It is not a logo.
- ▶ It is not your icon
- ▶ It is not your type faces
- ▶ It is not brand guidelines.
- ▶ It is not your ADS
- ▶ It is not your colours.
- ▶ It is not your YouTube channel.
- ▶ It is not your shop front.
- ▶ It is not what your CEO thinks it is. Or anyone else on the board for that matter.

In many ways it's all of these things, combined to create an impression of what the consumer thinks you are.

Let me say that again.

**It is more about what the consumer thinks you are, than what you think you are yourselves.**

Let's discuss more.

Over the years I have worked with businesses of all shapes and sizes. I'd say at least 90% of the time I have used the word 'brand', their eyes have glazed over. The wallets closed shut and the conversation nosedives.

So, I started changing the word. Instead of talking about 'brand', I talked about the 'personality' of the business. Once I sat with a client and chatted around the concept of a business having personality, they totally got it. It's weird isn't it that a word like 'brand' can scare the living shit out of a client? Maybe it's just one of those buzzwords that gets overused and then loses its meaning.

Anyway, let's get back to personality.

I'm going to tell you a little story that hopefully explains why personality (brand) is so important for your business.

In the spirit of not offending anyone, this is simply a description or a possible event in a bar or club. It could even be on a train. The characters and their sexual preferences can of course be anything/anyone/any type.

Imagine you are in a club or bar. And you spot somebody who you fancy or who takes your eye. You look, they catch your glance. You look again and they look at you again. This goes on and on. The blood rushes to your head. You can sense that they are interested in you. You certainly are with them. So, it's clear that you are attracted to each other. In other words, you fancy the look of each other. Bingo.

You end up chatting and getting to know each other a little. And you like each other. The way they talk, the way they sit and all kinds of other little things that make you like them. There may be more. You see each other again and bang, the relationship is more long-term. The point is, there is attraction.

This is not dissimilar to how people see brands.

There is an attraction.

## Selling propositions

Welcome to the USP, ESP and VSP

**So, what is a USP?**

A USP is a Unique Selling Proposition. Quite simply, it means what it says on the tin, it's communicating something unique about your business, product or service.

The only problem is there is very little left in the world that is unique and, like the idea of an everlasting light bulb, it doesn't really exist. Although, I am sure there are businesses out there that do have products and services that have a point of difference. Just not unique.

It all comes down to whether you think you have an edge against your competition.

It's your choice and your decision but be damn sure you're clear about what you're saying and why, otherwise "Percy Punter" will see right through it.

Take the ad industry for example. Most agencies offer pretty much the same thing; creative, account management, strategy, artwork, insight, research and so on. There's nothing unique about these services is there? Some agencies may think the way they do them is different, but that's not necessarily unique. You need to think carefully.

There are value propositions. VSP's

I personally find these are non-starter. Why? Because value (used as a key driver in marketing) to something makes it feel a bit transactional for me personally. Yes, I get the idea that something brings value to your life, or to your business. They typically solve a problem that you are experiencing within your life or business, however, I'd much rather utilise them alongside some emotions. Then you have a real hook.

They communicate things such as "It makes XYZ quicker", typically a lot of these can be software based or SaaS based as value propositions nowadays.

But for me they do feel one-dimensional. I do think they have a place lower down the hierarchy within the communications. More on this later.

What is of far more interest to me (and many of your customers, although they may not realise it) is what we call an ESP—Emotional Selling Proposition. Emotional selling propositions do exactly as they say. They play on the emotions of people.

Many brands forget to do this. The good ones don't.

In a nutshell, unique selling propositions are difficult to come by, value propositions are transactional by their very nature, whereas emotional selling propositions tap into people's emotions.

As I said, for me ESP is the winner hands down, every day of the week; it is the most important tool any brand can use in its advertising and marketing. Why? Because we are all human.

The use of emotions is King. We're not robots. We are made up of a complex web of experiences: nurture, nature, environment, friends, family, good times, bad times, relationships, you name it; everything humans go through, we are emotional beings.

When I see ads for double glazing, that tells me it's buy one get one free I think, "great, cheap double glazing". But it's not the reason I'm actually buying it. There could be many reasons, let's take a look.

If I stop the draft, I stay warm and I feel more comfortable. These are things that make me **feel** nice. The keyword being feel. It might be that I want to get double glazing because

I've got old windows that look rubbish and let all the cold in. Yes these are practical reasons. But me imagining being sat there with my nice new shiny windows and problem solved is a more emotional one than a practical one. I **feel** good about everything. At the heart it's emotional drivers that make people go yes or no. The value/price may help support the message. Not the other way around. Yes I might want it for 50% less, but I'm not going to buy it just because it's 50% less. The emotional aspect is often the tipping point. We've probably post rationalised that we want something. So tap into those emotions.

I used to work on the ad account for a major sofa company in the UK, and as you can guess everything was half price. There was always a sale. However, for me it's not necessarily the offer that makes me want to buy the product. If the sofa looks like a giant tampon, no amount of half price and money off is going to make me buy the horrible looking thing.

It's the same with a car. BMW could offer me half price but if I don't like BMW's, I won't buy one. I have to like the product (emotional). I have to have a need for the product (value proposition). And I have to feel I can afford the product (price).

And there it is in the right order. Why waste good ad spend and real estate communicating price first or value first?

Sell me the sizzle (as an old colleague said).

There is a need to have an emotional connection to want the product or service, so, if the sofa means I can sit back on a

Friday night, with my Chinese and a glass of red wine on my new comfy sofa, then that's an emotional reason for me to want the product. It's about my lifestyle and what I 'want'! Half price is just a bonus if I happen to like it, it's the same with the car. If I happen to like BMW's and I want to feel like I'm driving a nice car AND the offer is there, then bingo, the emotional connection with the reasoning.

Emotional selling propositions have helped produce some of the best advertising that has ever been done (and results) as they have tapped into an emotional psyche: our needs, our fears, our hopes, our dreams and our desires.

When it is done correctly and underpinned with other values it succeeds. Unfortunately, most advertising nowadays is emotionless, or surface at best. Especially on social media platforms.

There appears to be no want or deep rooted need to understand our customers. A real desire to create meaningful communications is what aligns our products and services with their needs.

Instead we simply pump out a whole load of crap on social media in particular (as well as TV and other marketing comms) that shouts, tells and yells rather than connecting in a deeper way. No wonder brands are seen as big greedy corporations. Don't get me wrong, many brands do some great work, but the lesson here is, do you really think about what your customers' needs are?

The thing is, I've talked about brands being about personality.

Remember the story about fancying somebody in a bar? Those laws of attraction and ultimately choosing to stay with somebody for a long-term relationship. Think about the windows and cars and sofas. If you just saw them based on price without emotion, it's just a transaction, there is no long-term value. Whereby selling with emotion means you're being attracted, being understood, being engaged with and being talked to rather than talked at. All these things help build better long-term relationships and, ultimately, better lifetime value between brands and the customers.

Maybe I'm going on, but I hope you get my point here.

How many of us really want to be in a relationship with somebody lacking completely in personality?

They may even look great, but it won't be very satisfying in the long term. For me in life, in a world full of businesses and brands that connect with us on a daily basis, it's no different.

It all comes down to how they talk to us, which is mostly inward looking. Look at us, look at this, look at that. Not how it helps you.

Most businesses are so inward looking that they simply communicate benefits rather than the emotional benefit of what they solve.

This takes me nicely on to talk about customer pain points.

Consumer pain points.

One of the biggest things to understand about your customers is their pain points. What's causing them grief or problems?

This is one of the most pertinent questions you can ask anyone.
- Why?
- Why are you having this problem?
- Why are you encountering this issue?
- What problem are you having?

Because straight off the bat it shows you have empathy. That you want to be able to offer value, whether that comes in the shape of help, assistance, a product or service that helps take that pain away for them.

More great questions to ask are:
- What will happen if they don't solve the problem?
- How big a problem will it become?
- What effect will it have on their lives?

I think you get the idea. It's all about asking the right kind of questions. Questions based around why they have a particular feeling, emotion, problem or challenge; because at least we hope your product, service or brand will help solve their problem.

Asking questions is simply one of the best things we can do as marketeers. And as people. Simply put. Listening.

Trying to really understand customers is key to everything. We've talked about putting ourselves in the customer's shoes and part of that is trying to understand the nuances of their lives and also understand their pain points.

That's because if your product or service solves the problem and takes away their pain, they are more likely to buy it. Regardless of how good the ads are or how well targeted they are, if they don't fundamentally communicate that they solve a problem or take away somebody's pain point, then why would they buy?

Please don't mis-understand, I'm not talking about negativity here. I'm simply exploring the realms on why people will buy something or not. I've talked about the use of half price propositions and whilst that's fine to a degree, it's not the only thing that needs to be communicated. One could argue that it takes away the pain point of people not having the money, they would like to buy a new sofa and that half-price offering makes it more affordable. This is, I agree, taking away a pain point for the customer. However, utilising emotions is far more effective. If my existing sofa is falling apart, or I think I want a new one because I've redecorated my room, emotional things are in play. So we really need to understand how products or services solve these pain points as well.

It can make you feel more at home, more settled once your room is fully finished. My pain point is that having redecorated my old sofa is bringing down the look of the room and nullifying all my hard work. So, a new sofa makes it complete. That solves my needs. Not just the half price. I would rather see half price sofa ads aimed at first time buyers. That does solve a pain point! But if I have oodles of money, it's a different pain point. This comes back to understanding our customers and what their lives are like.

This is where YouTube is quite simply brilliant. Consumers can spend hours in front of different markets at different times, but when they have intent, and the inclination for your product or service is in the forefront of their mind, YouTube allows us to place ads in front of them, not other folk who may not be that fussed.

We are also now all traceable, we can see all the data that we need. So, we can run our half price sofa ads in front of people, who have been on Rightmove or various house building sites. How cool is that?!

We also know that they are in the market for the sofa, we know they are interested in a sofa and we know they're likely to be quite tight for money, so we could even run it in front of the properties to which the value of the sofa is more aligned. For example, running ads for half price sofas to those we know are first time buyers, as opposed to running ads for luxury sofas in areas where average income is higher. They may have completely different pain points, the first time buyers just need a sofa, whereas the owners who already have a nice pad in their 50s may just want to show off to their friends, but each customer has their own specific pain point and that can be utilised. I'm sure you get the idea.

Understand the customer, understand their lives, understand the pain point and then get a proper agency, one that knows what the hell they're doing, to create the ads with the right targeting. This way you will get the right things in front of the right people and bingo! The results will begin to show.

## Using emotion

Far too many brands just trot out inward and dull communications. They think their product or service is amazing. They think it's the best thing since sliced bread and that everybody wants it.

As a side note, I wish I had a pound for every time a client told me, when I asked the question, "who is your target market" and they replied "everyone, everywhere". What a joke.

Anyway, back to things about dull communications. How many ads can you try and remember? How many posters or newspaper ads can you recall? How many bits of advertising came through the door that made you jump up and go show your partner or kids how cool it was. How many social posts do you show your mates? The answer is probably not many. Yes, I can remember some great TV ads over the time and some amazing ads and posters, but most of it is pants. In my view there is a simple reason why most of it is boring, irrelevant and poorly made advertising.

What most of it lacks is any punch and kick, or for want of a better word, any "emotional" fuel. They simply tend to state something rather pedestrian and dull. The answer is that we do remember when ads pull our emotional strings. Whether that be funny, exciting, fear inducing, humorous or sad, they tapped into something that resonated and that helps us remember.

When we use emotion and advertising, we are using the most powerful tool that we can. At the end of the day, we are not robots, we are humans and we want to be entertained, we want to feel alive, we want to laugh, cry or whatever else it may be. We want to feel like we're living.

So, when brands utilise emotions, it hooks us in and grabs our attention, it involves us. Or to use the latest buzzword, it 'engages' us. The average consumer in the UK is bombarded with 6,000—10,000 messages a day which is insane. I reckon it's even more if we take into account social media and the sheer number of hours most of us spend on it. This is really scary. It's scarier for brands as they are wasting their money on their communications, because quite frankly, out of 10,000 messages a day, how many do we remember and what they have to say? I'd hazard a guess not many. So, this creates a problem when we talk about ROI, awareness, reach, impact and all those lovely buzzwords that we throw about all the time. The truth is your message is getting lost, your communications are perhaps grey in the eyes of the customer and not really standing out in the mountain of content and advertising crap.

- In 2007 the average person in the UK saw approx **5,000** ads a day compared to 2021 where that rose to **6,000-10,000** ads a day
- In 2015 digital ad spend was **$156bn**. In 2020 it doubled to **$299bn**.
- Facebook was formed in 2004
- YouTube was formed in 2005
- Twitter was formed in 2006
- Over 50% of global ad spend was digital in 2020

So now you see the problem—most of it is dull but, by using emotion and tapping into how your customers really feel, is by far the most effective way to communicate and produce amazing results, brilliant awareness and ultimately drive business success long-term.

One of my favourite quotes is by Bill Bernback, the man who helped set up DDB, one of the world's leading agencies (in my humble opinion). In fact, many people see him as 'the greatest ad man of all time'.

Also, look up some of his quotes as they're sure to inspire even 50 years later and teach people a few things about advertising and indeed business in general.

"Be provocative. But be sure your provocativeness stems from your product. You are not right if in your ad you stand a man on his head just to get attention. You are right if you have him on his head to show how your product keeps things from falling out of his pockets."

Bill Bernbach

So, whilst I bang on about using emotions, it's also really important to make sure they are relevant to our customer base and who we think our customers are.

The following actually happened to me, whilst in a fairly dark and sensitive place emotionally, after the passing of my father. Something you may relate to. A local social media company started promoting the use of video on Facebook and other such channels. One of the examples was for the local funeral directors and in their infinite wisdom, decided to use a cartoon animation. You know one of those off the shelf jobbies where everything looks the same as everybody else who uses it? My issue wasn't with using a cartoon necessarily, my issue was using it for a funeral director. You've just lost a loved one and you're saying I should use their services via what looked like a jokey cartoon?

This is the totally wrong way to use emotion. Moreover, it just made me think that the funeral directors, as a client, was fucking stupid. How insensitive even thinking it was appropriate! I wouldn't mind if they had used a flip psychological idea to make a very, very good point but they didn't—it was dog shit and I was offended.

Now I would never use that brand or business. I am just one customer of course, but my reaction could be felt by many in a similar place and this careless form of advertising could cost customers. Whilst I'm banging on about using emotion you have to be 100% careful when and how you use it. The right way to do it is to know and understand your customer, you absolutely need to empathise with their situation.

Therein lies two of the most important factors in advertising, emotion and empathy. Some may say they are one and the same, but it is all about knowing the right way to use both and to not carry yourself in a way that could negatively affect your brand. That comes down to understanding and having empathy with who you are talking to. In fact, to me emotion and empathy are the two most important words in marketing. In my mind, ESP stands for both the emotional selling proposition and empathy selling proposition. This helps you avoid what the funeral directors did. It simply makes you align the emotional trigger with the needs/desires of the customer.

This segues nicely on to understanding our customers.

## Understanding our customers

I hear and see so many posts and articles written about understanding your customers as if it's some new-fangled, marketing, God-like insight. It simply makes me chuckle (and angry when people look up to these people like they are revealing some amazing thing in marketing).

It's one of the core things you are taught to do way back in the day. A guiding principle that's always been in the ad industry.

As a 'wet behind the ear creative' many years ago, I was taught it is the first thing to truly understand, on any creative brief for any communications. I can hear now, Charlie saying, "*Put yourself in the shoes of the customers and not the client, because it's the customers who pay the client's bills*". The client will always view things from their own perspective. They don't buy the product. The customer does. So, when coming up with ideas, you'd best make sure those ideas resonate with the consumer. Does it emotionally prick their ears, does it touch a nerve, does it understand what their needs are and does the product or service resolve those needs? Your ads need to reflect this and communicate the USP/ESP. It's not about what I think as a creative either. It's about creating ideas that float your customers' boat ultimately.

Many years ago, I used to teach in colleges as a visiting expert lecturer. One day I took in a new brief. The brief was for Saga Holidays and it was simple enough—come up with a 48-sheet poster idea, to promote a selection of holiday destinations for the following summer. This to me, was a great brief, the students didn't think as such, so they sighed and grunted because it was an old person's brief. I told them to calm down and crack on. I knew what was going to happen and it was making me chuckle deep inside. The target market was basically 50+ year old men and women, couples, singles looking for holidays next year. The brief clearly stated the destinations and the types of holiday they were. These included going hiking, sightseeing, horse riding, generally doing interesting and activity-based stuff.

I was considered a bit of a hard taskmaster because I didn't teach lectures, the whole point was I was running it like a professional ad agency studio. I would review ideas at the end of the day not in 6-weeks-time, which was the norm. It came as no surprise that they had done ideas that they thought were right and not what they thought the target market would respond to. Their ideas were appalling and horrifying, in the ways that made the old people look like they were virtually on their deathbeds. Too old to do anything interesting. Their ideas were sedentary in terms of the visual language. For example, people sat on comfy loungers and people sat by pools drinking tea (I kid you not!). Fundamentally, they misunderstood what it was like to be somebody 50+ who wanted an interesting holiday. They assumed that all people over 40 were old and needed a zimmer frame and didn't do anything interesting with their lives and that they all just sat around drinking tea all day. So, I let them go home that day thinking they were correct.

The day after I took in around 20 pairs of shoes.

These included:
- Sandals
- Smart shoes
- High heels
- Flip flops
- Walking boots
- Trainers
- Wellies

Both in male and female versions, there were varieties of all of these types of footwear. So, as you can imagine, there was a lot of choice.

I laid them all out on the table and then asked them to write down what type of people would wear these shoes. Their age, name and their job.

They complained, this was a distraction from them continuing with their ideas on the Saga holiday brief. So, I made them moan even more when told to put all their ideas they had done the day before in the bin. I simply told them that they were way off the brief and that this next exercise would change the way they view people forever.

So, after much moaning, they binned their ideas and started writing down which type of person would wear each individual shoe. I knew exactly what they were going to write down and it made me chuckle even more deep inside.

For example:
- The sandal wearers are born-again Christians in their 50s, 'God botherers' as some of them wrote.
- The ones that wear the wellies are in their 60s and work on the land—farmers.
- Smart shoes are for somebody in the city—mid to late 20s, a sharp, business-hungry type.
- High heels belonged (rather disparagingly) someone they thought was a bit tarty in their 30s.

You get the idea.

You should have seen their faces when I told them that they belonged to me and my wife. Every single pair. It's fair to say at this point my wife was a senior lecturer in this college and they all knew her really well. They were horrified and begged me not to tell her that they thought she was a tart, a Christian, and Farmer Giles.

It was hilarious.

I then made a very important point that they had assumed their target market lived and behaved in a certain way, so when I talked about putting yourself in the shoes of the customers, they had not done that. Yes, this was a bit of a silly game, but it did make a great point.

So, I told them to write down what life was like for the people in the Saga brief when they were in their 20s and 30s. The era that these so called 'old fuddy-duddy types' lived in is what's now known as the 'swingin' 60s', and what happened then? A sexual revolution of course! Sex, drugs and rock and roll music, cultural changes, the likes of which we'll probably never seen again. I made them think what these people were really like and what they're like now. I also pointed out that the brief clearly stated that these potential customers were active during holidays rather than sedentary. There was a silence in the room, and I sent them off packing to redo all their ideas. I reminded them to put themselves in the shoes of the target market (the customers) and write ads that would excite them if they were in their 50s, having grown up in the 60s, wanting a holiday that was a bit more adventurous, rather than sedentary.

I think you know what happened next. Within 2-days they created ads that were bang on. There were some crackers.

After that whenever I gave another brief to the students, they always made sure they put themselves in the shoes of the customers and really understood what these people were like. In fact, we got to the stage where they would debate as mini teams what the lives of people would be like. Their interests, the things they watched, the things they listened to, the way they would take it all in (any ads they would see). This ensured that the ads talked in a relevant and creative way to the target market. The student work at the end of that year was simply excellent and a lot of the ads they produced were on par and, in my humble opinion, better than some of the students who already had degrees, despite them being 3 years younger.

My point is this. Understanding your customer and putting yourself in their shoes is the most important part of the creative process. So, even now when we do YouTube ads, one of the key parts of our briefing sessions and discovery sessions is getting the client to work with us on the customer profiles, in a detailed and insightful way, that allows us to target and write YouTube ads that truly resonate with the customers they are aimed at.

That may seem obvious to say but it's so fundamental. It's also talked about as if it's some new-fangled thing. Which properly winds me up.

## Truth in ads

My old college lecturers would ram down our throats, many things to help shape us into flourishing young creatives.

These lecturers were amongst the very best in the UK. They had taught some of the best (as in most students went on to work in the very best ad agencies and had great careers). It wasn't a degree, but an HND and it was highly regarded in the qualifications in the UK at that point, 30 odd years ago.

They themselves, had worked in the top agencies and had learned from some of the best in the industry.

So, there was a good *'blood line'* so to speak.

I/we trusted them with whatever they said. We hung on their every word. They would often back it up with reference to the industry greats such as 'Bernbach' and 'Ogilvy'. Some of which I will share soon.

One of the things that was driven home the hardest was that, regardless of how creative an ad was (which was a given that it would be highly creative), it still had to be rooted in truth.

I think you might be thinking what the hell am I on about.

Well it's simple really. Creativity for creativity's sake is wrong. I'm not talking about fine art, culture and music here by the way, where the gloves are off. I'm talking about the ad industry and the commercial aspect of creating ads. If (and many creative people are guilty of this) they just want to make some crazy headline, mad picture or pretty image because they think it's nice, quirky, or controversial, then they are wrong.

Why?

Because it's not based on delivering the truth of the product or service.

Here is one of favourite quotes by the late great Bill Bernbach:

# "The most powerful element in advertising is the truth."

Bill Bernbach

Creativity is more powerful when based on the truth.

It magnifies it in the right way.

And consumers are not as daft as we think.

Too many communications and ads are based on flippant ideas. Rather than some true and core thought. Ultimately if you do ideas that are not based on the truth, consumers will not trust you and the relationship is broken. They won't come back to you. They won't believe in what you're selling, and they will go elsewhere for that product or service. To a place where they believe someone is telling the truth about what they're offering.

To this end it simply means you must build your brand mission, vision, values and proposition based on the truth of who you are. Authenticity is key and King.

And you know what I'm going to say next, don't you? YouTube is the best place for brands to be authentic and truthful to who they really are. People go to YouTube because they believe that over and above any other platform it's where people go for help/assistance and a more authentic experience—so what your brand puts in front of people there needs to mirror this. The way YouTube allows you to personally target its user base with adverts means those ads require even more care and attention because those seeing them will have been selected as a potential customer for your product/service. This means it's important not to alienate them with shitty and irrelevant advertising!

When they are done correctly, ads on YouTube can be very powerful and really resonate with the customer base. The best ads will show your message and your core values; this is important because, as stated previously, your brand is a personality and if that personality is fake, then customers will see right through.

## Why creativity is key

Creativity is a funny old thing. In 30 years of doing this I would say 90% of the time clients don't see any value in it. And I'm not just talking about small clients here, I'm talking about some seriously big brands and businesses. They approach it with scepticism and dismiss it as a fluffy, esoteric, non-essential business thing. Don't get me wrong. I talked before about creativity for creativity's sake and that we probably have not helped ourselves as an industry, by trying to be wild and wacky whilst not being relevant to the consumer's needs. So, it's no wonder many clients have a distrust of it and don't always believe when we show a great idea, with strong convictions, that it's the right thing to do.

But the world has certainly changed in terms of the digital era. Things are far more trackable, and we can demonstrate good ROI. The problem is most communications on the digital platforms are lazy creatively and data-driven and they still work really well. They don't really need to employ any creativity. They can just get a message in front of the customer base and it will work enough to give a decent return that the client thinks it's the best thing they've ever seen. Without much effort. It's become the norm and it's lazy. Simply trot out usual copy lines and ideas, stick it with some broad, brush stroke targeting and away you go. It will work to a degree as I said. That is changing though!

It is lazy. And just like creativity for creativity's sake, this 'spray and pray' approach is also not doing the industry any favours. Many clients don't always believe their PPC reports and SEO reports and all that other bullshit that runs out the back of the system, saying the data looks really good.

Here is an example (I know Simon has briefly mentioned this but I'd like to dig a bit deeper).

One of our clients was involved in time and attendance software.

They were running a PPC campaign.

On Google Search page one, there were maybe fourteen results. The top three or four were paid, the rest were organic and there were a couple of paid ads at the bottom.

All of them pretty much said the same thing. Time and attendance software.

So, rather than being lazy and doing the usual we employed a little bit of creativity in our approach.

We decided to put ourselves in the shoes of customers.

You're starting to see a picture here?

We realised the pain points for these potential customers is that people were late for work and it was difficult to track them sometimes. This was costing them time and money.

So, we did something that we don't think anybody has ever done before on a PPC campaign. We wrote the ad with a pain point in it.

The ad said, "Oh dear, Sarah is late for work again!" Maybe you need to consider (company name) time and attendance software.

It worked a storm. Why?

Because...
- It stood out
- It was relevant
- It touched upon a pain point
- It embraced emotion
- It had a solution

All in 20 odd words.

All because we approached the task in a creative way.

I could give many more examples of where creativity has made a huge difference to the success of a campaign. I've always approached it based on telling the truth and what the product or service does (starting to see a pattern here?).

For me creativity is central to everything we do. Without creativity I wouldn't be typing on a laptop, I wouldn't be able to boil a kettle to make coffee.

It is central to society and it is central to business and its success.

It is not some afterthought.

It is *the* thought.

Especially when we talk about marketing and advertising, creativity is fundamental. It's just how we use it and apply it, that's the question. And when done right it unequivocally brings more success to the clients marketing campaigns.

The great thing about YouTube is that the targeting is so immense that it allows us to put really creative ads, in front of different types of people in really easy ways, that truly resonates with them. I would also say creativity is subjective and very personal.

What one person thinks is creative, the next person may not, and vice versa. I think this is where you then need to employ the services of extremely insightful ad industry creatives and agencies, who understand how to manipulate ideas to the very best of what they can be. It is a rare skill. One which takes time, craft, understanding and a mastery of viewing the world and the things around it in an unlimited (blinkered free) way.

## Why it's authentic and the way forward for ALL brands and business

When you run an ad in a newspaper, it's clear it's an ad. It's very difficult to get around the fact that the reader knows it's an ad. It is.

When that sales leaflet falls through your door. You know it's trying to sell you something. It's got a big red sale on the front.

When you hear a radio ad, it's an ad.

When you see a TV ad, it's an ad.

The point is they are all clearly ads. You might think I'm being a bit thick here but, bear with me.

By the very nature of the mediums, they are created as a make-believe world. Think of the 'Bisto' mum. Happy families in the kitchen. Same with the beautifully art directed and crafted photograph on the magazine ad. It's a world of make believe. It's not real. The radio ad is a land of make believe again.

Don't get me wrong, there are some amazing communications and I'm not dissing them at all. I'm just merely pointing out that they are a "created" and "false" representation.

All sparkly and glitzy.

On the other hand, YouTube isn't.

You had people at the start, and still do, so post "real" life stuff.

People search YouTube to find out how to do something. Rewire a plug, cook a certain recipe, change a part on a car.

They search it for real and authentic stuff.

People posting gym techniques, Yoga classes, the list goes on.

People giving advice.

People visit to find new music, real bands. The one you saw at the local boozer last Friday.

So much of it is real.

And for this reason, you can also experience the brand on the platform being more real too. Real staff, real factory visits.

It's as if the veil has been lifted.

And this is amazing.

If, as a brand you are a bit scared of showing the real you, take note. You will fall behind your competitors.

If, on the other hand, you embrace this new world of 'real' people, wanting more 'real experiences', then your business and brand can go out there on YouTube and be authentic. Punters love this.

It's not trying to be an ad. It's not glitzy, it's not under the veil of some ad man's tricks.

It's the real you. The real deal and the real business.

People believe you more and build more rapport with the brands that are acting like a real family, rather than a made up one on TV (*caveat—Bisto ads worked great and in the ideal world you'd do both!*)

So, yes, still do the other marketing. But also embrace the new world of authenticity online. Your punters will love you for it.

I also think though, that you have to be absolutely clear what you stand for. What's your DNA, your mission, your vision and your values? If you don't have them nailed and don't portray and live by them on YouTube, you'll get caught out.

If you can be true, consistent, and bring value, you'll succeed, and it will deliver results unlike any other medium.

### What's your customer thinking?

Who knows! Do you? Do I?
- We can use insights.
- We can use research.
- We can even talk to customers.
- We can second guess.

In the old days we would second guess. Yes, second guess. There was a lot of skill, insight and research done. A lot of very clever people all stewing over what a customer might really be like and what they might be thinking. A favourite of mine on a brief is, *"how do we want them to feel when they have seen the communication piece?"*

It's all guess work. Because we don't know.

BUT.

We do know a lot more nowadays.

Every search we do is logged. Every website we visit is logged. How long we have spent on this page, that page, is logged. What we bought. What we added to the basket but didn't buy.

What we paid for on our debit cards at the supermarket or shop. That data will exist somewhere.

Someone, somewhere, will know that the weather was 29 degrees and sunny at 5.31pm on Friday the 7th June in Retford; and that I bought two bottles of white wine and some ice from Asda.

Something, somewhere will work out that it was bought because it was a nice summer evening.

Google will know that I'd looked at garden chairs two days before and that I visited the Argos site because I'm tight and wanted two cheap camp chairs. It will know I didn't buy them. It will know that I searched several others and didn't buy, as

I kept clicking off the expensive ones. Somewhere someone will know I bought two from Asda on the Thursday before the Friday on an offer of 2 for £10.

Someone, something, somewhere knows all about us.

What we eat. What we buy. What we watch. What we listen to. What we drink. What we search for. What we desire. What we fantasise about.

Even what we talk about. Yes, they do listen. Simon has talked about us being listened to. That absolutely has been collected.

So, they know all about us.

After all of this, this section is titled **'What's your customer thinking?'**

Well, let's be honest we know an awful lot. Of course.

But here is the killer.

The one thing they do not know about is...

**Why?**

Why did I buy it? Why do I watch it? Why do I desire it? Why do I prefer that drink to the other one?

Why?

Because AI and all these programs still can't do what humans do. We still need humans to understand humans.

So, all the tech in the world still needs us at this point in time.

Remember that saying?

*What you get out of the machine is only as good as what you put in.*

Put shit in. Get shit out.

And that's exactly the same with YouTube ads.

Poor targeting, placement and buying.

Poor result.

Great targeting, placement and buying.

Great result.

Humans. We know how to do it. Our tech makes it better, yes, but it's our skill, wisdom, integrity, understanding and knowledge that decide what we put in the machine.

Only we can work out the maybe of 'why'.

## Your Domain, value in the brand (putting it on the balance sheet)

Are we all not somewhat dependent on our domain name? 'Symbolics.com' was the first internet domain name, registered on 15 March 1985. Since then, there have been hundreds of millions of domains registered worldwide. The question therefore is 'what's the value of a domain name?'

None of us own our domain, they are effectively on lease from the registrars. The thing is, if your domain is known, generates great traffic, sells your product, allows potential customers to contact you, then clearly it has value.

As an ex-accountant, it fascinates me that domain names still don't appear on a balance sheet as a company asset. The reason? I believe it is purely because accountants don't know how to place a value on a domain.

We need to look at a domain in terms of 'brand'. The danger is that a domain can become so valuable that a business could collapse without it. Imagine that you're a business taking 100s or 1000s of orders a day through your website, your customers have bookmarked your site and your site comes up for lots of generic search terms in Google. Of course, that domain has enormous value—were that domain to expire and your website disappear, then the business would collapse overnight. It's clear that a domain can have a massive value to a business, so why not put a value on it and put it on your balance sheet?

Our domain *www.s.media* is a single character domain. There aren't many of those for obvious reasons, and if you search 'single character domains' on Google you can find the Wiki where most of the single character domains are listed. Indeed most of the single character domains never came to the market for fear that they would be exploited, so there are even fewer than you might think.

So, why am I rattling on about domain names and their value? I firmly believe that as you, as a business, build your domain in search you are adding value. Imagine that a competitor comes to buy you out, but you sell the company and say to them "*But we are keeping the domain...*" The company goes from worth something to worth potentially nothing, so that domain or set of domains should clearly be on the company balance sheet.

By the way, if you are an accountant reading this, I'd love to debate the value in domains and capitalising them onto the balance sheet.

The reason I want to talk about domains and their value leads us into the future of marketing. Google is favouring video marketing, favouring Q&A and puts enormous weight onto the resources that allow its searchers to discover knowledge.

In the main that knowledge base is stored on domains, those domains link the fabric of the entire web ecosystem together. Links have always been a really valuable indicator for Google of the power and therefore where it ranks a domain or page within its search engine. There are of course businesses which only exist on social platforms and don't necessarily even have a website, but the overwhelming majority of businesses will have a website.

Nowadays link building is a little old hat in terms of search engine optimisation. Google prefers 'social signals' and engagement metrics for ranking, in which those social signals come in the form of likes, comments, shares, reviews, etc. What better way to drive engagement than video? YouTube is owned by Google and it is pushing video. If there is a takeaway from this book, I'd like it to be that those of you who have taken in most of the information, go forth and build a great YouTube channel. Done correctly YouTube videos can jump to the top of search within 24 hours of being published. You can't do that with a web page!

Now, once you have a great social media presence and YouTube channel, go ask your accountant to stick a value on that! The answer you will get, I imagine, will be similar to the one I received—"*You can't put that on the balance sheet*", or can you?

An influencer without their channel—worthless, no exposure, no reach. I'm sure their accountant, were they selling their business, could come up with a figure. This all hangs off the 'brand', but that brand is supported by its component parts. ITV for example would not exist without its channel, that channel has value. Do you see where I am going with this?

I found an article where it stated that as of 2020 there have been 605 sales of single-character domain names with an average price of $23,700. About 70% of the single-character domain name sales were in country-code domain extensions. The top sale was Z.com at $6.7 million. Elon Musk originally owned X.com, one of the world's first online banks, which eventually became PayPal in 2001. Try telling the accountant that domain has no value! The domain itself X.com directs nowhere! Very odd that it is just sitting there doing nothing. Here is the Whois:

*Raw Whois Data*
*Domain Name: x.com*
*Registry Domain ID: 1026563_DOMAIN_COM-VRSN*
*Registrar WHOIS Server: whois.godaddy.com*
*Registrar URL: http://www.godaddy.com*
*Updated Date: 2017-07-05T21:02:43Z*
*Creation Date: 1993-04-02T05:00:00Z*
*Registrar Registration Expiration Date:*
*2026-10-20T19:56:17Z*
*Registrar: GoDaddy.com, LLC*

The domain expires in 2026!

In theory this domain not being in use could be sold. What would someone pay for it? It clearly has a value. Personally it amazes me that Mr Musk doesn't at least direct it to his SpaceX.com domain. Ho hum, I presume though he has other things on his mind and the odd few million here or there doesn't concern him! Dear Mr Musk, if you are reading this and have no further use for that domain feel free to let me have it, I am sure I can put it to good use (or just stick it on my balance sheet at $10M)!

The point of this section of the book is to look at your domain as an asset. When publishing video and social media posts, think of your domain as the central hub of your own internet. Your domain is there to help Google understand your business footprint online, linking all your assets together will add value to your brand, and this is the future of SEO.

Yes, AEO (answer engine optimisation) is coming and may well in the future replace the text-based search engines we see today (that is where Microsoft is heading). That's not to say that Google will disappear, no, what will happen is Google will use more and more video, more Q&A and continue to push towards a thought-based query engine with true AI.

That's a few years off yet… or is it? The lesson? Get making video, make sure you link it to all your social channels, make that video interesting and engaging and answer questions, be helpful and inspiring. After all, the phrase 'content is king' has never been so true, but now we need to make a slight adjustment to that. 'Interesting and engaging content is more valuable'.

And something to leave you with…

In today's online world, a business is fundamentally nothing without its domain. It's inextricably linked.

Very.co.uk

Apple.com

Jet2.com

I could go on.

They reckon the brand element of Apple accounts for 50% of market capitalisation.

I wonder what the domain is now worth considering it may have been available at $10 back in the day? ∎

# ▶| SEO | Simon

## SEO is brand

▶ Lots has been written about SEO becoming brand. Let me explain and give an example.

If you have a successful business and all the traffic to the website is based on paid CPC and you have little or no organic traffic from Google, other search engines, or social media, then your business could be extremely vulnerable. Not just from competitors outbidding you, but when, and if, a potential purchaser of your business comes forward and undertakes their due diligence, they will find it would be extremely easy to potentially replicate everything. The very least that will happen in that scenario will be a lesser valuation of your business. All they need to do is spin up a website and set up the ads (yes this doesn't take into consideration that you may have a very unique and hard to source product or service).

However, the point I am trying to get across is that on the flip side, if you have a massive footprint in the search engines, tons of backlinks built up over the years, active social media accounts, followers and product evangelists, then it is going to be far harder for a potential investor or purchaser to replicate what you have built. Therefore, SEO equates to brand value.

SEO positions contribute massively to the value of any business in that respect.

The issue with an SEO strategy is initially the question of affordability and risk. Over the years, having been in SEO since the very beginnings of the web and studied in depth both on the dark and light sides (there are still plenty of shady SEO tactics being used by agencies), I've come to the conclusion that probably 95% of the SEO industry either doesn't really care about their clients or is selling a product they fundamentally don't understand.

It's a continual frustration seeing companies paying for SEO when the search terms their agencies are trying to rank them for are invaluable. By that I mean even if they did reach No.1 in Google, they'd not break even once you take the cost of the campaign away. Back in 2017 I wrote a 'constructive rant' on LinkedIn predicting the end of the SEO industry, pointing to the fact that many agencies in the space were akin to pirates—sailing down the high street stealing fees from clients who just didn't understand what they were buying (or the lack of work that was going into their campaigns from the agencies they had employed). Here's a snippet from that article as it still applies today and generated a great deal of debate in the industry.

### *"Death of the SEO Industry, it needs a clean-up*

*Watch out! There's a thief about—and it's most likely to be your SEO agency! It is most definitely time the industry was cleaned up, is it time we took out the trash and got rid of the fraudsters that are all too common?*

*I will tell you what 'ails' me. Dirty Freebooting companies are living the dream while breaking the bow of the ship they are supposed to tug, taking its booty and sailing away while it sinks.*

Ok, let's talk Search Engine Optimization—the 'real thing' not the muck pedalled by web designers or IT guys. Trouble is most people who think they are SEO experts don't even know the half of what can/should be done, even 95% of SEO agencies are frauds (not knowingly), they just don't have enough genuine knowledge. They haven't put in the research and done the hard hours, they are selling something that doesn't yield long term results and hence gives the industry a bad name.

I feel qualified to talk about the subject, as I have built my experience and expertise in SEO, more so than most in the field. Since the very beginning of my career, I have worked with the web and developed websites always with SEO in mind (not as an afterthought). I have learned something to do with SEO almost every day for the last 25 years.

Having always held a fascination with SEO, I can tell you with confidence that driving websites to the top of search has been the difference between the life and death of my business and for many of my customers over the years. When my competition lagged behind and fell by the wayside, it was my passion and determination that drove me to the high standards of excellence I still hold myself to today.

My love affair with web design and SEO began in the bedroom in 1994. I designed my first web pages in basic HTML and played around with simple programming tasks. While others got into designing games (I later came to wish I had, perhaps I would be retired by now) I was hooked on building websites, and the challenge of pushing more visits to my web pages. My romance with SEO was beginning. Even today my team will be heard saying 'Oh no, his autistic side has come out again' when I find another tool or fascinating technique!

All search engines have one goal; 'find and organise data sources on the internet for the benefit of their users'. Before the dawning of Google and the coming of Bill Gates, the Internet was a barren desert made of File Transfer Protocols (henceforth afterwards referred to as FTP), which users would traverse with the assistance of newspapers, books, relevant links and word of mouth acting as the stars in the night sky, from which users could plot a course to their desired data. Like the north star, Polaris rising in the darkness to help weary travellers on their path, Google has grown to become the dominant navigational marker of a constantly changing digital road. The world of search is changing—I wonder if there are other search engines that will surpass Google in the future. Microsoft is very determined, watch this space, Bing is on the up for sure—especially with results for paid clients driving conversions as it seems more affordable than Google currently.

It was not always this way. As the central list of web servers joining the Internet grew, and the World Wide Web was becoming the interface of choice to start navigating the digital desert (which, by this point was and rapidly growing to become an online ocean), the concept of a search engine began to take off in 1994-95 with a man. A man named Alan, good old Alan. He had vision.

In 1990 Alan Emtage, a student at the University of McGill in Montreal created Archie. Archie was an index (or archive) of computer files stored on anonymous FTP websites (I wonder what he is doing now? Maybe he should have called it Google?), which was the start of something new and incredible in the industry. It would take a long time to go through every search engine I have seen the rise and drop of in my career (many have fallen to the wayside, forgotten) so below is a brief insight into the history of search engines from my perspective

**Excite:** Born in 1993, it was the first to use statistical analysis to improve search relevancy. Bought in 2004 by Ask, Excite now offer PPC & Natural search listing.

**Yahoo:** Born in 1994, Yahoo initially employed personnel to organise and categorise its listings until 2002, when they moved to a crawler-based system. In 2004, Yahoo purchased Overture, Altavista, Alltheweb, and Inktomi.

**Webcrawler:** Born in 1994, it was the first search engine to provide a full-text search feature. It was later sold to excite in 1997 and merged in 2001.

**Overture:** Born in 1998, Overture is considered the pioneer of paid search. It was purchased by Yahoo! In 2003.

**AllTheWeb:** Born in 1999, Overture bought Alltheweb in 2003 and was rolled into Yahoo!

**Lycos:** Born in 1994, it was at one time the world's biggest search index with over 60 million documents in 1996.

**Infoseek:** Born in 1994, it was one of the first to introduce Boolean search modifiers. In 1998 it was bought by Disney corporation now it is mostly used in North America under the name Go.com

**Altavista:** Born in 1995, near the end of 2002 it became the first search engine to offer Image, audio, and video as part of a multimedia search before being purchased by Yahoo in 2004.

**Inktomi:** Born in 1996, it was sold out to Yahoo in 2003 for $235 million.

**Ask Jeeves:** Born in 1997, Initially popular, Ask is now struggling to compete with Google, Bing, Baidu, MSN and Yahoo.

**Google:** Born in 1996, the heavyweight champion of search engines was created as a school project at Stamford University. It began life as BackRub, before later being renamed to Google, when Google Incorporated was founded in 1998.

**MSN:** Born in 1998, MSN was renamed to Windows Live Search in 2006.

In those days the digital battlefield of the world wide web was a wasteland, devoid of tactical direction but equally lacking in a dominant competitor. Relevancy was everything for the search engines and is still the number 1 concern for Google to this day. Personalization of results, reviews and recommendations are all a major part of modern search algorithms. AI is now coming to the fore, where will it take us next?

Everyone always says 'content is king', but I challenge that idea. Yes, before you assault me with angry comments and berate me, I agree that content is a key point in any business website creation and a central spoke to the wheel, but relevancy & engagement are more important to the search engines and will become more and more critical over the next couple of years. Your content could be the finest vintage wine in the world, but nobody is going to taste it if the search engines conclude that too many users are bouncing off it, not tempted to engage or talk about it.

A large quantity of irrelevant content clicks results in a high bounce rate, which in turn will contribute to giving you a lower search ranking over time. With Google's mobile-first algorithm update already rolled out, you have to think about user experience. This is where Google won the search engine wars and became king of the digital hill.

So, back to my bedroom 20+ years ago and the beginning of my affair. It was relatively easy in those days to rank websites, and I remember well checking Lycos, Ask Jeeves, Altavista and Infoseek regularly, before Google swaggered onto the centre stage. Maybe it is because I am a bit of a geek at heart, but I felt incredibly powerful and a sense of immense satisfaction seeing my websites shine at the top spots. When I was listed at number 1 out of thousands and sometimes tens of thousands of results, I'd like to say I wasn't really concerned with the competition. However, whenever somebody did appear above me I would sit all night and often into the early hours of the morning researching, building links, writing content and building pages amongst other things. Nobody was going to be taking MY top spots.

Hindsight is a beautiful thing. Obviously, I was fighting a losing battle for some search terms; I did at one time rank a website No.1 on Google for the word 'bank' just because I wanted to know if I could do it, LOL :) If only I had known where things were going to go back then. Another missed opportunity to be retired by now! An experience I would later use to push my career further into the field of digital marketing, SEO and now AEO.

Fast forward a few more years, a group of friends working in IT decided to start their own distribution business. I had the opportunity to build the website and run the SEO campaigns, and this was an incredibly successful venture. Within two years we had a business turning over £6 million with 20 employees, life was great. We were even finalists in Young Entrepreneur of the Year, on the TV and in the newspapers.

It was at this point I probably took my eye off the ball for a while regarding SEO. It was all too easy when we were driving Porsches and Ferraris (Looking back I should not have let myself get distracted so easily).

As the business grew, so too did the money coming in. People began to get greedy; tensions rose until eventually I fell out with my then partners and decided to go it alone starting from scratch.

*I left the company, partners, Porsches, and people behind to begin my new venture, again in IT but this time instead of selling to the trade, I went for the end-user market and started an e-commerce business. It was back to the drawing board, and I have to be honest, this is what I love about the web and SEO—an opportunity exists everywhere.*

### The Algo

*Algorithm updates are a daily occurrence within Google, and they keep a tight lid on the actual mechanisms that crunch through the data to provide our current search results. It is a constantly evolving field, and many companies still refuse to stay on top of the latest developments in cutting-edge SEO (more on this later). Social media plays an enormous part in what we do nowadays; many so-called 'SEO experts' don't believe in social signals, they, therefore, don't deserve even to put SEO in their job description in my opinion.*

*I had to build my rankings again, and quickly. I was prepared to put in the hard hours required (It was the early 2000's). We did well. I spent the majority of my time working on SEO and websites, gaining many 1st rank listings (above many national brands), a huge online presence and building a network of contacts. I had the experience behind me to make it happen.*

*This was before eBay, eBuyer, and Amazon arrived on scene. The real big boys weighed into the markets I was targeting, buying the same products I had access to (although I am pleased to say that we were often above them for our chosen keywords), but with their buying power they were able to drop and maintain prices below ours and we struggled to compete by 2010. 2012 came, I sold the business to a competitor as a going concern and was headhunted for a big agency working on national brand accounts.*

*The love affair that began in the bedroom back in 1994 continues to this day, much to my wife's amusement. SEO has been a constant companion, coupled with a real passion for Social Media and creative marketing. I have been in bed with e-commerce, search engines, B2B, PPC, National Brand and experienced everything in between the covers, yet SEO continues to surprise me, and I learn something new every day.*

*I now run my own full-service web, digital, and marketing agency and I am also one of the UK's top experts on LinkedIn social selling. We have SEO specialists who report to me, learn from me and collaborate on tactics; I hold my team to the same standards of excellence that I began with. Many young people who have worked for me have gone on to work for national brands in their marketing departments. Whether they are experts in the field of design, web, branding, creative, PPC, PR etc. my team provides a fully comprehensive digital service that I am proud to lead."*

So, what's the issue?

The point of this article is that certain companies and so-called 'specialists' in the field of SEO are rubbing me the wrong way. Yes, I am 'blowing my own trumpet' here, but I truly believe there are very few people with my level of experience. There should really be a recognised SEO qualification—99% of agencies out there that claim to 'know SEO' would fail any test I set. I recently commented on a LinkedIn post, you know, the ones where someone is asking for a recommendation for an SEO expert to work with. The post immediately filled up with comments suggesting people that could be of use, agencies spouting rubbish like "We are here to help!" and other such spiels.

I hate that.

The good old 'SEO Recipe'

I especially hate the fact that none of these people have anything different to say or offer, they all peddle the '*good old SEO recipe*' and treat it like a game. They may as well be an alchemist in the middle ages selling potions '*guaranteed to cure what ails you*' on the streets without giving out a recipe or a result to back up their boasting. The problem is, business owners are not equipped to discern between one SEO company and another, many have had their fingers burned many times and been left with a bad taste in their mouth.

We've all seen it before; posts, blogs, and emails stating "*I can get your business to the top of Google!*" or "*Beat the competition, be ranked No. 1 in search with our help!*". Yet when it doesn't work out, you've spent thousands and the answer is "*Oh, give it a few more months, these things take time!*" or "*you need to spend more to see more results*" and my personal favourite "*It's not our fault, Google must have changed the algorithms*". I smell something, and it's not pleasant.

The comment I made in the post was something like this—"*Who here has a point of difference? Can anyone show me their tactics and prove they are the cutting edge of SEO?*" The silence was deafening and telling. None of these 'professional' SEO guys were able to give me an answer, show any evidence or strategies they would use for a client.

This is what I like to call the 'Smoke & Mirrors' effect; many SEO 'veterans' peddle a standard recipe of deceit, repetition, and expenses. A little knowledge is a dangerous thing, and many of these guys charge extortionate prices for 'research' and 'hours spent on-site SEO' etc. but they do not report what they are actually doing.

Let's move onto the actual experts in the field. I do train quite a few agencies in good SEO techniques, passing on my knowledge. These agencies like to bring me back again and again as they know I bring something new every time. Most people who do have a good knowledge of SEO don't get off the hook so easily either; sitting at the cutting edge hoarding secrets and huddling quietly in the corner conversing in hushed whispers, lest a rival agency snatches it away and use it against them. To an extent I can understand. I hold my own IP when it comes to SEO, and my notes about the latest developments and tactics are secured safely in an Indiana Jones style brown leather-bound journal that I keep close to heart. But the world of SEO changes weekly. I have sat with some of the directors of the biggest companies in the UK who are very successful in terms of sales, yet limited in knowledge.

One example, in particular, comes to mind. I was at a meeting with the technical lead at a SEO business not far away from me where I asked the question "*What about social media and its use for SEO?*" to be told that, and I quote, "*there is no link between social media and SEO rankings*". I nearly fell out of my chair, said good luck to them and told the client I was representing to walk!

Another misconception amongst business owners is that SEO is a technical task. Therefore, it should be given to the

IT department (big mistake) or presume that every web-designer is SEO proficient.

Massively WRONG! While you may, and I stress, MAY be able to get some SEO out of a web-designer (I happen to know a few in the field that are excellent), your man or woman that handles printer support and networking is very unlikely to be able to tackle the complexity that is SEO. Ask yourself this, "Is SEO their major area of interest, is it their passion and is it the way they earn their living?"

SEO is a massive beast, 95% of people who claim to know SEO will tell you about tools like MOZ, SEMRush etc. They will talk about META TAGS, keyword density, blogging and errors on your website plus link building... that's maybe 10% of the game.

I've recently published a free to access SEO basics course. It's nothing spectacular, but it will give you lots of ideas of how SEO should be done. It will also encourage you to ask your SEO professional (if you are using one) some pertinent questions and see if they truly are running meaningful campaigns for your business. It can be accessed here (you have to register but it's got 13 short videos you can watch): *https://institution.s.media/*

## A little knowledge

It is a misconception that everyone who says that they are an SEO expert actually is one. This is an incredibly costly error to make. Nowhere else is the saying '*A little knowledge is a dangerous thing*' more relevant, and lots of these people may have some knowledge about SEO, filling in the gap with Google. I know how to build a small wall out of bricks and mortar in my garden, but would you call me a builder? I know how to use a spreadsheet and add up columns, I also know what a profit and loss statement is—would you call me a qualified accountant? NO, NO, NO. Please get rid of that guy who's a friend of a friend who 'knows SEO' because he managed to rank a website a few years back—the game has changed, you need a pro.

This is the same scenario as your web-designer or tech-support employee claiming they know about SEO. It is a completely different skill-set so if they cannot back up such claims with evidence, steer clear and hire a real professional team to build your results and prove an ROI.

As for professional teams, make certain they walk you through the process. Then, unless they can guarantee tangible results, please demand access to statistics you can trust; data with date ranges and numbers, segmented for your target audiences, etc. It is not unreasonable for a client to ask to be walked through one simple request: *"Show me what you have done with evidence that your work has made me a sale"*—You pay them to do this! Then drop them if they won't or begin to squirm. Too many SEO companies just send a weekly or monthly report with some annotations—don't you deserve a little more than that?

I see this all the time, day in, day out, clients coming to us who show me a lovely report their so-called SEO company produced for them claiming it took them hours. Trust me, don't pay for SEO reports, most SEO software auto-generates one for each client and it takes the click of a mouse.

## Where does this leave us?
Well...

I can tell you that myself and my team would be able to provide you with the details and evidence of our work, to back up any claims we make and more importantly, demonstrate a very clear ROI through our detailed analysis and reporting insights. As a policy, we take on only work we believe in and clients who want to truly dominate their markets, we never lie to our clients by providing false data. You should be able to trust your digital marketing company to do the same. We all work in this exciting field together, and I am sure that many of my colleagues in the field have become equally frustrated with the current trend of businesses taking advantage of those who know only enough to bluff their way into money—talk is indeed cheap!

I have worked incredibly hard in my long love affair with SEO to build this castle, and although I will not return to the bedroom again to do battle like it is 1994, I do have an office now plus a young and brilliant team of staff I'm responsible for and often work late into the night on behalf of clients to gain top rankings. I can tell you with confidence, I will not let my standards of excellence be tarnished because other companies are being sleazy, taking money for little or no effort.

## A clean-up is in order

I suggest a clean-up is in order. Let's take out the trash and restore faith in SEO and the Digital Marketing profession.

Now if you excuse me, I think I hear my life calling. Apologies for the rant, perhaps I should have titled the article: *'Sack your SEO company and get a decent Marketing Agency on board'*. SEO is not what we sell, it's a consequence of all the hard work, content, strategy, planning and research we do. Does your SEO agency offer all that?

I'd be really interested to hear from you online, about what you think of SEO agencies. Have you had your fingers burned in the past? Do you think the industry needs cleaning up and standards-setting? Have you tried the agencies from abroad only to find your rankings slipping and getting hit by Google updates? It's all out there and 95% of them are thieves and fraudsters... thoughts?

I'd encourage you to take my free SEO course—*SEO basics course—Free* there are some questions in there that you should be asking your SEO partners for sure.

Here's a recent video of me talking about AEO and SEO— *https://youtu.be/HPAETR6hAPk*

Ask your SEO company if they are planning campaigns for AEO. If you don't get an enthusiastic answer then it's time to walk and find another partner. Likewise, if all you feel you are getting is a monthly report for your money, be worried!

## SO, what's the future for SEO

Video and questions, that is the answer. Google wants all the answers, as do all the search engines. Answers follow the question and those sites that solve users' problems retain traffic and provide a useful resource—meaning Google et al. We already see '*Other people asked*' as one of the most important and prominent sections on the first page. To get your site into this section if you have an SEO goal is one of the most valuable positions you can have. 95% of the sites featured in the Q&A section on Google currently have a text based answer and link back to their site. More and more though we are seeing videos popping into this section and the future is undoubtedly that this section of search will be dominated by video and voice. After all, who wants to read anything anymore and there is the old adage that a 'picture tells a thousand words'.

One of the issues is though that for now most SEO companies wouldn't have a clue or the will to take the time to try and rank in the Q&A section.

Take a step to the side and have a look further into the future—Google, Microsoft, Amazon, Facebook, Bing, Apple etc. They all have their plans to provide a proper fully functional and engaging voice search. There is a real race to the top going on and all we need to do is think where they are getting all their data from. Look far into the future and this knowledge and assistance will come out of androids, home help systems and lead us into a completely different world (hopefully not the one where Skylab takes over, and we all know where that ends LOL). As I write we have tools like Alexa, Cortana, Siri, Bixby and Google Home, but none of them provide a particularly engaging or seamless experience, certainly not one close to where we will be in the future.

If you're reading this and want one of the best pieces of advice you will get for an SEO strategy, it would be to research all the questions your potential customer asks about your product, the challenges your product solves and the future of your industry. Get that nailed and publish the right content to answer them via video and voice and you'll win out long term over your competitors—but it will need consistent effort and commitment.

As stated, SEO has everything to do with brand now, that means building social signals and coverage across as many channels as possible. I've been very outspoken about SEO and effort vs cost and benefit. It's a sad day when a client signs an SEO agreement with an agency and said agency isn't going to produce an ROI report on a monthly basis, and by that, I mean a clear statement of the achievements with the resulting bottom line improvements clearly associated with that activity. As far as I can see there are literally zero agencies which do that for their clients. Yes, they will say X search term has moved up Y positions and give a strategy as to what are the plans to move forward, but what does that mean for the client in terms of revenue? The SEO industry has to be one of the only industries where clients don't actually know what they are buying or paying for and the associated benefits, it literally is the epitome of 'selling the dream'. TOSH

It's clear all search engines are moving from text to video and voice. Social media obviously has an enormous impact on search marketing, as well, social signals and primarily retention and engagement are the main ones to pay attention to as a marketeer/brand. What is, therefore, the best strategy for the future?

Videos that are informative, answer questions, and that are subtitled so search engines can also pick up that content (as a side note always use as many of the tools Google etc. provide and don't get lazy). Then get them shared as widely as possible, promote them, gain as big an audience as possible AND make sure that is the right audience so that retention is high. All of that will result in your content being ranked highly for your chosen audience.

Here's an example of making sure you are ranking for the right audience and the right keywords.

A former client of mine was a commercial window spraying business, in which their previous agency had spent months and thousands of pounds making efforts to rank the client for 'window spraying'—sounds great right? Wrong. Looking at the competition, the client literally had next to no chance of outranking competition for that term. They then employed a paid strategy and targeted the same term. What they forgot was (and this should be obvious) to exclude the term UPVC.

Searches including that term were all end users (homeowners) and completely irrelevant to the business. By simply not including UPVC as a negative search term in their campaign they were wasting 95% of the client budget. Again this seems obvious, but laziness and lack of thought resulted in appalling results, a client that lost their belief in the whole process and thousands of pounds and months wasted. The best part? The campaign was being run by a very well-known and so-called 'expert agency'.

Bottom line here is though, by choosing the wrong terms and by sending the wrong traffic, bounce rates on the pages went up significantly and the rankings suffered massively as retention/engagement was down. No wonder many clients lose their belief in the process, again it is all too easy to get it wrong. With the wrong audience and wrong search term the targeting was wrong and therefore, the whole campaign failed.

A far better strategy for the client was to answer all the questions surrounding the commercial side of window spraying and do that in video format. Getting people to watch is then easy, with a combination of paid ads with very specific keywords and building highly targeted audiences. The catch-22 is that without the traffic the retention and engagement on the content cannot be measured by Google and therefore you don't rank. So think of paid search as a tool to drive traffic to your content, get it noticed and then ranked. Long term you can then look to rank organically, and again, that can be measured, tracked and the ROI calculated. It's incredibly frustrating seeing great content being made and then nobody seeing it or the wrong audiences seeing it, which in turn leads to damage SEO results for the piece of content that could have conceivably ranked No.1

## Edutainment

Let me frame this a certain other way.
- There's only so much you can say and communicate in a 30-second TV commercial.

- There is only so much you can say and communicate on a 48-sheet poster, that people drive 30 miles an hour past on a daily basis.
- There is only so much you can communicate on the 60-second radio ad
- There is only so much you can say on a full-page newspaper advertisement
- There is only so much you can say 1200 pixels Square online ad

And there is an old saying about *"don't throw the kitchen sink at it"*—as in don't try to say too much.

I couldn't agree with this more. I've given many talks about keeping it simple and stupid. People can only take so much in at any given time. Say something well and say it once.

However..

There is a new way of doing things. And this is YouTube.

It gives you this amazing gift. **Everything** and **Everything**!

Awareness, lots of CTA's, educational opportunities, entertainment, tips, advice and so much more.

And it can be as long as you want. Why? Firstly, because you only pay if someone takes an action or watches more than 30 seconds, and secondly because if the targeting is correct then the right people see it and they will want to watch. Yes, there are some sweet spots from our learnings (such as 2-3 mins in length). The great thing is you can do all sorts and

communication things within this given timeframe of your choice.
- ▶ get a hook in
- ▶ use emotion
- ▶ educate
- ▶ a clear CTA (call to action) in
- ▶ testimonials
- ▶ product demonstrations
- ▶ awareness
- ▶ almost say anything you want!

Any order, any which way.

It does all this and so much more. And you can see where people have fallen off, to help gather insight on retention rates and really dig deep and understand how people have watched the videos. In massive detail as well.

We have created videos that are really technical, with close ups of how to do things. We have created some that are more entertaining and attention grabbing. Some have been shortened. Some quicker. We've done animations, graphics, live actions, a mix, close ups, wide angles, to camera, off camera and action stuff.

The possibilities to entertain, educate and everything else in between are endless. ∎

# ▶ Video Killed the ********* | Simon

▶ It's a new world order out there—video and YouTube Ads.

Google said that it envisaged video being the no.1 consumed content on the web and it is right, literally nobody wants to really read anymore online. My own team came to me this week and talked about our blogging strategy for a new site we are launching. My response was *"who put us in a time machine and took us back 10 years?"*. If there is one thing that you can learn from this book it will be to make video the first consideration of marketing campaigns going forward and stop wasting time blogging (I can hear the SEO 'experts' out there mumbling, but trust me, I'm right), watch or read?

I know what 99% of the population will choose, and video is ranking now a lot more quickly in search than blogs—why spend 100s of hours and months of work SEOing pages and optimising meta tags, building links, creating social signals and spending thousands with agencies etc. when you can rank videos at the top of search engines pretty much within a few days?

The opportunity is now, that's because video used to be perceived (and still is to some extent) as expensive to make, yes you've got to come up with a content plan, create a brief, a script, storyboard, go film, edit, subtitle, add meta and descriptions, upload and then promote.

It's a lot to do, but as we can now see from creators, production values don't have to be massively high (we aren't making a Hollywood movie or TV special). This can be another barrier to entry as the people in charge of budgets often perceive the finished product in their mind to be just that and stop at the point they think 'we can never make what I want'. Creators now have mobile phones capable of great TV quality video recording. Yes you are going to need light (outside works well as there is often this thing called 'The Sun') but failing that lights are really cheap now. The bit that lets a lot of amateur/semi-professional videos down is the sound quality—again, bob onto Jeffco and buy a half decent microphone and you are good to go.

Getting back to the opportunity though, we're still at a point where the budget holders are what I would describe largely as the *'non believers'*. These are those people who didn't grow up reliant on the internet (some would call them lucky) but as society becomes more and more dependent on technology and a daily immersion into the web, more and more marketing pros and budget decision makers will be able to spend on video. But that's not right now. So as we have seen above, video is still perceived as expensive, the planning is time consuming, people worry *'it will not be good enough'* and then there is the real biggie... *'I don't want to go on camera'*—that's the real challenge for many.

So, there lies the opportunity, Google WANTS video, it prefers good, easily digestible content over pages that people find boring. Remember the mantra of Google, browsers must find what they are looking for, be engaged. They can't find pages that aren't engaging, they must under no circumstances for even a blink of an eye consider using an alternative search engine—heavens help us if someone mentions the word BING!

Bottom line is there is a massive, enormous, gargantuan opportunity, and that's video. Once the next generation gets into more senior positions let's look at what is going to happen. They are not afraid to go on camera, they've grown up with social media, they know what works in terms of content and they will not hesitate to produce the content that they know will work. That point may only be a couple of years away, it might be 5, but I don't think it will be as far away as 2030, no chance. So, brands that don't wake up and start producing decent video content and lots of it, will be swept aside by newer brands run by younger execs who know the power of video.

## How did YouTube gain its advantage?

Google announced that YouTube made $15 billion in advertising revenue in 2019. Something Facebook and other social channels struggle to achieve is the monetisation of their content, and YouTube is giving a slice of the pie to its creators.

Many influencers make huge amounts of money from their channels—the incentive is enormous, and the production values don't have to be very high to gain an audience and therefore channel subscribers.

One of the biggest mistakes many brands are making is the assumption that 'only kids are watching YouTube' or '40+

guys' (as an example) aren't watching. We are talking about a medium that attracts more viewers than TV and is set to grow exponentially.

As YouTube incentivises content creation through monetary reward as well as allowing video to pop up more and more in search, brands need to pay attention.

Not to make money from views (leave that to the fame craving self-absorbed, and let's be frank, the crazies out there), but as the perfect product placement opportunity. Put a product someone has searched for, who is in the target demographic or even on one of your competitors websites or apps at the right time of day? Literally magic! Measure the conversions and come to an EXACT cost of acquisition of a customer, something you can't do with TV, and you never will be able to. Will TV advertising become a thing of the past? No, but it will have to become a lot smarter.

## What wins on YouTube

Audience retention is the key to unlocking the chance to appear as a suggested channel, or video on YouTube and therefore, the massive view numbers that come with it. Retention is trying and achieving as high a percentage watch time as you can. The further through your video the average watcher goes the higher the retention rate, this will mean you outrank your competitors and get viewers to convert into business.

The higher your video retention, the more likely you are to pop up in the 'suggested content' and this is where a ton of the traffic comes from. YouTube CARES massively about retention—they want people to stay and watch.

Think about it, the better the video, the more people watch, the more YouTube will reward you. This is like old school SEO but for video, then the more people watch, the more your video is rewarded.

Remember that your video is competing against millions of people uploading similar content. Yes there are 'tags' you can enter, you can have an awesome description and links to your video BUT, retention is king. Every person is sending signals back to YouTube. How long do they watch, are they pausing and going back and re-watching interesting bits? Are they sharing, commenting, liking etc? But the real game is to get them to watch your video, all of it if possible.

Target other people's videos—connect other like-minded partnered channels, work together with other influencers and collaborative channels. By collaborating with influencers you are also as a brand able to offer them the opportunity for you to buy all their advertising inventory, they get more views, they make more money, you advance their careers and they get super excited at these types of opportunities.

You can even then link up channels into your ads accounts and retarget users that have, for example, been on their channel in the last 30, 60 or 90 days. One of the really big evolutions on YouTube will be the collaborative opportunities and as brands learn this more and more influencers in tighter and tighter niches will benefit, as they bring in advertising dollars and also revenue from brands wanting their audiences.

Layering audiences—job titles will evolve over the next few years, audience specialists will become a real thing (if they are not already) and people with real insight into what it takes to design and maintain audiences will be massively in demand. After all, small variations in audience are already the difference between enormous success and horrendous failure.

Placement into certain channels. You can of course chase placements and you can choose which channels all your ads are placed into. Some people still love this as a tactic and it does have its use, however it's a little old hat now. The issue being that the opportunities are limited as well as the impression numbers.

Better tactics are to layer audiences and bring into the equation 'who someone is' while overlaying 'what they are searching for'—then you have something that Facebook for example doesn't. Yes the AI behind Facebook is ridiculously clever and perhaps this is where WhatsApp and Messenger help (they are listening and profiling), but maybe there is a privacy problem in future—who knows with that one?

What we do know is that the targeting on Google (and therefore YouTube) have far more data points than Facebook can ever achieve, also YouTube has a bigger footprint. As I write yes, Facebook has the bigger user numbers on a daily basis but a smaller retention in terms of eyeballs per day (YouTube average watch time 30—40 minutes a day, Facebook under 15 minutes)

Use social proof to increase watch length and retention. By getting involved with other influencers, it is possible to gather more social proof, meaning that trust is built up and therefore, you achieve a longer watch length and retention score. This leads to ranking higher and becoming a suggested video, gaining more impressions and so the roll up begins to becoming preferred content.

Competitions work well in the space. Asking for subscribers, likes, comments off the back of prizes, especially from influencers, can mobilise their fan base and get them to watch longer.

When something goes viral, join in the conversation and make your comments and respond with 'news jacking' style opinion.

## The Barriers to Entry—Beware

So, where do we stand right now? With businesses getting themselves onto YouTube slowly and starting out, it's still a misconception that you need an active YouTube channel in order to run ads. The actual facts are that all you need is a channel and the video you intend to use as your advert to get going.

Remember though, make that video have the right hooks and calls to action, make it as engaging as possible and people will click through, subscribe, watch, comment, share—basically all the good stuff!

One of the main issues and maybe something that is perhaps slightly generational, still revolves around business owners who aren't brought up making video.

As I speak, I'm sitting here during lockdown, which is lockdown 3 in the UK, and pretty much every business on the planet has been forced into video communication tools like Zoom, Google Hangouts or Microsoft Teams.

Maybe everyone will come out the other side of this with more confidence to make video and get in front of the camera. Personally I think that is still going to be a major barrier to entry, let's face it there is a whole world of difference between chatting online one to one and trying to make a piece of creative content.

I'm sure more and more people are going to let themselves get on screen and show their personalities, but still business owners think that the barrier to entry is making the video in the first place. There certainly is a challenge, they don't necessarily want to go on camera, they don't know what the content should be—all of these things can be addressed reasonably easily.

When we start talking about what the content your business could or should be making it's important to remember you're not attempting to script and create the next Hollywood Blockbuster, win a BAFTA or even impress your competitors. You should concentrate on making a video that speaks to your audience clearly and makes them trust you as a source of information.

You need to make sure your video is 1 to 3 minutes long (and ideally longer in many instances). These video ads need to convert and get people to click through or take action. Your first thought should always be the audience, will they watch?

Will they engage? The higher the engagement the better the advert and content is going to perform now and long term.

Business owners need to worry about those new exciting and dynamic entrepreneurs, the switched on marketeers, or maybe those that are reading this book. Business owners need to worry about those businesses that are springing up after lockdown run by professionals in their 20's/30's who have no qualms about putting themselves in front of the camera, that are not shy, who get the fact that video is the now and know it gives them an incredible advantage.

I listened to a podcast very recently where I heard Rand Fishkin, the founder of MOZ, talking enthusiastically about 'brand' being the future of SEO, not link building. He's 100% right, getting your brand out there and your content out there is so important and first mover advantage means that if you make the content (and by that I mean quality, engaging and valuable content) first, that is where links come from and that is where your video will be linked to. As the creator within your niche you have the ability to then be linked to, engaged with, and are seen as the authority.

All of this can happen very quickly, it's time for lots of business owners to wise up and see video as the future of SEO and brand. Putting it off isn't going to wash, being shy isn't going to wash, using some stock footage and a voiceover, guess what? That isn't going to do the trick either.

Worry if you are in the Old Guard, those businesses that prior to lockdown were struggling to make video and are still not interested in making video, who suffer from procrastination, can't get a clear strategy in place for video production and content aligned to driving new engagement on social media.

I've talked about it many times and I still laugh to this day. I sat in a board meeting with a client and we were presented with an SEO strategy which didn't include video or social media. The SEO agency in question didn't believe social media had anything to do with SEO—those are the dinosaurs I'm talking about.

Many businesses that fall into the 'Old Guard' category are going to find very, very quickly that the younger more dynamic agile businesses come along producing video, jumping into their market and grabbing those customers in the blink of an eye.

We've seen results ranking videos for clients in the last 2 weeks that have gone straight into the top of Google search. The transformation of search results based on video is happening more quickly every day, more quickly than 99.9% of SEO companies are realising. If you're stuck running normal PPC campaigns, you're going to find that video over the next year or two will dominate search, people will be coding videos with schema mark-up, adding transcripts to their web pages, blogs, podcasts, ranking videos based purely on engagement and not spending months building blogs and traditional SEO techniques.

Video will be coming up in the question and answer sessions on Google pretty much straight away and people will be collaborating across channels. It's these dynamic businesses that will engage with influencers, run ads alongside them and produce amazing content that people want to engage with that will win, and win big time.

It's not hard to imagine a world where we've given up searching on Google in terms of text, the only thing Google is worried about is voice search, Alexa being the prime candidate. Google sees video as the bridge between text and voice. It's not going to be very long at all before pretty much everybody is searching for and watching videos in order to answer their questions, this is inevitable.

It's almost already there on YouTube. The more businesses that jump in and make better content that satisfies queries, the more Google will serve it as a solution and an answer to someone's question.

The really interesting thing though is Google is able to obviously monitor how well audiences do engage with content (far more closely than we might think). Talking to a client today, I was explaining how we build their remarketing lists by creating videos that should interest their perfect audiences, but by only remarketing to people who watched over 80% of the initial videos. We were able to then make a specific offer to those interested and engaged potential customers—the take up rate of these types of structured campaigns was off the charts (instead of seeing conversions at 1 or 2% off the cold audiences, we were seeing 23%+ from the remarketing audiences).

So, it's really important to remember that it's not just how you make the video and what you put in it. It's building the right audience and when you remarket your offer that ultimately makes all the difference to the success or failure of campaigns.

Target the engagement, look for the signals that show you things such as watch-through percentage compared to click-through rate. If you are getting good watch-through, then great, but it's important to then monitor that people take action—if they are not, try calls to action at different points through the video (look out for bot activity though, this can show up as high view percentage and low CTR or the other way around, look out for anything that feels wrong and test it).

Video on YouTube is consumed far more than it is on Facebook. The absolute issue I have with the Facebook platform is, that in reality, you have a 'scroll and gone opportunity', that's besides the fact that Facebook and WhatsApp are listening to you and targeting based on your conversations (but that is a whole other privacy concern).

Video posted to your YouTube channel is effectively working for you forever, it appears in search, and when used as an advert someone has to watch 30 seconds or more to achieve a TrueView, that being the point at which you are charged as an advertiser. We often see videos that were posted to YouTube several years ago still featuring in search, you don't see that with Facebook.

Another interesting statistic is that video posted onto Facebook achieves about 11 to 12 minutes per day, per user average watch time. YouTube on the other hand, that same figure is over half an hour per user. Although YouTube doesn't have as many users as Facebook, it does have a significantly bigger use time. YouTube also has an advantage in that people are there to watch, Facebook users are there to be entertained or informed, post or engage with content that is not in the main video based, certainly not to be actively sold to.

YouTube is what we would call 'lean in', meaning that you have someone's full attention. They are there watching, and you are interrupting their viewing with an advert. They make a very quick decision and if they do choose to skip you don't pay, simple. Thanks YouTube, please don't ever change that model.

Another great example from another one of my clients following lots of testing—by adding a very low daily budget, say £3 or £4 per day, to every one of their videos that are published (a couple of videos each week), this guarantees them views and the video adverts are just there to drive the engagement and grow their audiences.

With a minimal budget they have built their remarketing lists to 10's of thousands of highly targeted potential customers. They know now that when they do spend the bigger budgets, very little is wasted and Google gets great signals in terms of engagement. They also have the side benefit that these videos rank in Google and YouTube as all of their videos are getting regular and targeted views.

This same client then retargeted all the viewers of the videos past 50% with one campaign, and viewers past 50% of the follow up videos with a further offer, then remarketed them on Facebook as well as YouTube and this created leads at under £0.50, quality leads.

The amount of video that is uploaded daily is growing exponentially. Facebook is maxed out to some extent, but the opportunities in YouTube can only increase as more and more content is uploaded, more and more interesting content goes up, more and more engaging content is produced, and more content creators become more creative and produce higher value productions. This in turn will keep the dross from the top of Google and YouTube—at long last top-quality creative will win, absolutely.

Please go and check out your competitors, are they making video? If they are not, the chances are you can steal a massive advantage, if only you can make the shift and commit to a video based strategic approach to marketing and SEO. Consistency and quality will win, couple that with commitment and you'll outrank competition very quickly. Don't be in the 'told you so' brigade, get making your video-based content strategy right now.

Although we can list other barriers to entry, cost should not be one of them. Pretty much everybody who's got a business these days has a mobile phone and those phones are able to record high level video really quickly.

There are plenty of apps out there which enable editing, subtitling and publishing. Some of the ones I like are Filmic Pro, Happyscribe, Teleprompter, Movavi and Zubtitle. Many, many more exist and *I am by no means affiliated with any of those I have just mentioned.*

It's really easy to have a video ready to go as an ad, pretty much within a couple of hours of filming, then simply edit it and upload it to your YouTube channel.

Promoting the content using Google Ads, it's easy to see that the cost element is not the barrier to entry. The actual barrier to entry is consistency and getting in front of the camera, making the commitment in the first place and not being too precious about how you look and the exact words you say.

Too often we see brands getting talked into alternative strategies, be that SEO or social media, PPC etc. their main reason being that they either don't know what to make in terms of video content, or if they do, shying away from getting themselves in front of the camera. We all hate seeing ourselves on video right? Well, get over yourself, your competitors aren't going to be worried about doing it and video will win in the search engines, so it's an absolute must.

We've been working with lots of brands who feel exactly the same as you may well do now reading this, we all know people who don't want to go in front of the camera and don't feel like their staff want to go in front of the camera either.

Often the marketing departments come and say let's 'have an animation' or an 'infographic', perhaps or we can find some awesome stock footage. People want to buy from people, fundamentally people want to look in the eyes of the people on a video and trust them. You can't get that from stock footage or animation (not to say besides the fact that animation is going to cost fortunes as well).

People want to interact with other people, feel the emotion and trust—look in the whites of your eyes, feel your enthusiasm. For that to happen the video needs to feel real, it also needs to be informative, educate the watcher, give them some value, and not just be a sales pitch. Consumers are turning off when faced with a pure 'sales pitch', nobody is tuning in to any content, let alone YouTube, to watch the adverts.

That said, one really, really, amazing tactic that works so well on YouTube is what we would call a 'pattern interrupt'. The pattern interrupt occurs when your potential customer is watching a piece of content they searched for, then your advert comes on and it almost doesn't feel to them like they're watching something different (let alone an advert), so it feels to the viewer like they jump straight from the content they were watching, and wanted to watch, to a more engaging and better piece of content.

I believe that this is where the truly creative agencies out there can make an enormous impact over the next couple of years. This alternative piece of content they are now viewing is actually an advert and constructed really to talk to the person, their intent, their emotion and targeted to get them to click through, take action and engage with your brand.

These pattern interrupt video ads can be placed into people's feeds at intervals which you, as the advertiser choose, picking the frequency of placement, how many times somebody sees an ad on a daily or weekly basis. One of the strategies I really like when it comes to impressions vs views is setting the impressions to 5 or 10 but limiting the views to 1 one a week.

That means that someone can keep seeing your adverts up to 29 seconds and therefore, the cost is zero for the impression, but then when they do view we are not paying to show them something they have already watched.

You can also choose to engage your viewers or your web visitors for a period, so for example you could choose to create audiences which are 7, 14, 30, 60, 90, 180, 360 or 540 days of web visitors or video watches. This is great, as we can therefore market to our engaged audiences for the right length of time, post first engagement, with some of our content.

This tactic is especially useful when combined with in-market and custom intent audiences having been overlaid with keywords and topics, producing a good quality first landing page visitor.

People who are engaging with your channel or website are already then added to your specific audiences, when you set this up inside Google Ads. It's all possible, there is so much opportunity with video that you don't get with traditional search, and as I've talked about in other parts of the book, the real gold comes when you can overlay who someone is, with what they're searching for, which websites they are visiting and what apps they are using etc.

Combining demographics, search behaviour on the Facebook platform is a bit more difficult. Facebook does use its AI to help track conversions and therefore, drive more of the same, and they can achieve extremely good conversions but, in my experience although the cost per conversion can be far lower on Facebook, the quality is lacking as the targeting is broader.

You make your choice, more numbers and more work, or lower, higher quality conversions from YouTube.

It's very difficult to imagine that in the long run Facebook will be able to compete with the way Google is able to target people. At some point privacy policy will restrict voice recording and monitoring I would imagine (although it would be denied I think), and there is enough evidence to point to the fact Facebook and its brother in arms, WhatsApp, are monitoring pretty much every word we speak into and in the presence of our mobile devices.

Google is pulling back on cookie-based monitoring and tackling the privacy debate before it gets out of hand; their defence is FLoC which is proposed to replace the current signals sent by third-party cookies. FLoC or 'Federated Learning of Cohorts' is Google's new proposition. They say that they are building a 'privacy-first' future for advertising on the web.

The death of the third-party cookie with its shadowy tracking is well overdue, but come on Google, we all know there are only a handful of winners here.

Google tells us that FLoC will see us all more protected in terms of privacy, I'd argue that this is just another way for Google to ring fence its position as top dog in the advertising space. FLoC is designed to help advertisers by grouping people with certain behaviours into cohorts. The future of the web is at a fork in the road here though, on a personal level I'd like a future where I get to choose the ads and preferences, but can that really happen?

I don't think so if Google has anything to do with it. FLoC seems to me to be Google putting a death grip on many of the unscrupulous third-party cookie tools which is great, but in the same breath making their job easier in order to profile people who are visiting certain sites and how they engage with content.

From the perspective of someone who uses the Google audience tools on a daily basis, this scares me.

We could conceivably reach a future where all audiences are built for us as advertisers and then anyone can use them. Yes, this simplifies the advertising process for all but it could take away the Google partners and a whole swathe of the advertising industry perhaps.

Maybe that is a doomsday scenario for the ads industry and far into the future, who knows. One thing is for sure though, with Google increasing its ability to serve ads to more defined audiences, I'd say as a brand, if you're reading this, now is the time to get into YouTube ads, now is the time to move away from other third-party advertising solutions, as their effectiveness is set to drop. Get on top of profiling your audience.

Google is going to be able to help you focus on who your perfect customer is, what they are doing online, which websites they are visiting and the moment of intent. You'll also want to look at who your competitors are, what apps they are using, what topics they are researching, what products are they buying, and it's not as limited as you may think.

You don't have to go after just the keywords that somebody is searching for, you can go after your competitors' customers by targeting audiences who've visited the login pages of other websites and apps.

This gives the opportunity to be very specific.

Within your campaigns you can specify ages, family make-up, and times of day, even income brackets in some locations. When we look at placing adverts at the right time of day into specific channels and against specific content, hopefully you see the possibilities, actually only ever serving your advert in front of somebody at the exact moment that you think they are ready to buy your product.

This is where Google wants it to end up, and with FLoC they are going to take huge steps toward that goal all hidden behind the curtain of supposedly protecting your privacy

## A picture paints a thousand words. So, what does video do?

Back in the day I used to love Art Directing long copy ads. I'd spend hours looking at D&AD annuals for the best work. How other creatives had crafted beautiful looking long copy ads.

I loved it.

I loved doing poster ideas. I remember doing ads for 48 sheets and 96 sheets (they were amazing to get a brief on)

or the more tricky format of a T side (bus side) or a simple 6 sheet (bus-shelter).

Double page spreads in the broadsheets (FT and the old Times) were such fun, and you really had to create amazing ideas to stand out. Plus it had to be a simple message. Pure in form.

Happy days.

And TV. It was always great to land TV briefs with decent budgets. Even better if the shoot was abroad!

But I'm reminiscing here, sorry.

There is a point to this section.

Words could cut through a hundred emotions like a laser when used right.

I've written both short copy ads of only a few words and longer copy ads with many words, winning awards for them.

I've equally created image-based ones that have won awards for their ability to visually strike a nerve.

But times have changed. It's been well written, documented and discussed that the long copy ad is dead.

People are lazy. They have the attention span of a gnat. They go about their lives a thousand mile an hour.

However, to be fair to them, they are bombarded with a billion messages every day from every corner. TV, digital, social media, Bloody everywhere to put it bluntly.

So, no wonder us advertising folk utilise every trick in the book to get their attention and hopefully get a positive reaction.

It's hard work.

So yes, a picture can help, but it's well documented, people don't have the time to read ads. People may still read (I believe you Taryn!). Of course they do, but on the whole they are still lazy and looking for a quick fix.

Most people can't be arsed and are not interested in reading your ads. Mind you, the occasional long copy comms piece can be really amazing at cutting through the noise, in the right circumstance.

Circumstance and context are key here.

There **is** a time and a place for:
- Long copy
- Short copy
- Image based
- Video based.

And sure, as eggs are eggs, video is on the rise. It's quick, it's easy and the lazy punter doesn't have to do anything other than watch it and then engage or not. No reading. No efforts. Just sit back on their arses and watch.

If they don't like the video they move on.

If they do like, they watch more.

And that's when the magic happens from an advertising perspective.

You see, unlike almost any other medium, video, and in particular YouTube, truly engages and builds rapport with your audience.

Get the targeting right and it is seen by the right people who will watch it.

You simply cannot say the same when the Corrie (UK soap opera for our friends overseas) break comes or you are reading a newspaper.

With video on YouTube you are telling a story, educating, entertaining, being funny, being sad, being relevant, teaching or even advising, whatever it may be. You can do this in one sitting. So, if a picture paints a thousand words, a video is like a mini-Hollywood Oscar winning movie, delivering the magic of brilliant advertising in a totally relevant way to your audience.

## What are Video Views Worth

We are still in the age of the influencer, views are worth money and YouTube has approximately 600 hours of footage uploaded to it every minute we exist. This is set to increase exponentially, so where does it stop?

Answer is, it doesn't.

As it stands, YouTube is dominant and Amazon is trying to get its foot in the door with Twitch and actively recruiting top influencers in the games space, to move from YouTube and paying them an enormous sum of money to bring their follower bases across. Twitch is amazing for live streaming and this may well be the way YouTube pushes its users (obviously there are plenty of live streams but it's not necessarily the main use of YouTube right now).

So, what is a view worth?

Currently YouTubers can expect to receive roughly £1000 for every million views, so that equates to around £0.001 or one tenth of one penny per view. YouTube itself makes at least 1p per view and a lot more when advertisers are vying for competitive keywords as well as niched down and extremely laser focused audiences. The more you target, the higher the cost per view. This leads us to the question of where will this all end up?

No limits to the volumes of uploads and no real limits to the amount of space available to place those adverts into. However, as the volume of video upload increases, the importance of quality production values increases. Do we move into a scenario where a primary and secondary system develops?

This already exists to a lesser extent. Advertisers with bigger budgets can afford to pay the rising cost per view and place their content in premium placements (and by that, I mean into competitive sectors), but currently the volumes of upload are exceeding (massively) the volume of adverts and advertisers. Until that balance is met and the mass adoption of video ads (breaking the barriers to entry), then the costs to advertise are likely not to rise much if at all.

YouTube is making 90%+ of its advertisers spend more and giving away very small percentages, and in most cases my 90% figure is a worst-case scenario for YouTube. Where advertisers for example are achieving an average 5p per view (as that seems as I write this, like a good benchmark), then in that scenario YouTube is giving away less than 1% of its revenue to channel owners. But still, channel owners who are achieving millions of views a week are making very healthy livings and that's besides the sponsorship deals, product endorsements and merch deals, where they can make absolute fortunes.

## Mission, Vision and Values. Why they are key to nail, especially on YouTube

If your brand doesn't have a clear mission, how can you expect your potential customers to buy into you? If you don't have a clear vision, how can you expect them to stay with you?

If you don't have a clear set of defined values, how can you expect them to even love what you are about in the first place?

And if you don't have a clear DNA (core identity) for all to see and connect with, how can you expect anyone to connect if they don't know what you stand for?

It's like changing the recipe every five minutes and what goes into it each time you see it. You'll never get famous for it and never attract clients back if you keep chopping and changing. They simply won't know what you stand for day in, day out.

You might get away with lazy mission, vision, values and DNA in certain marketing channels. But not YouTube. It's very important for everyone to see and comment. Get your shit sorted first.

I would say it's vitally important not just from a YouTube perspective, or indeed a marketing one. It's pretty much fundamental to your entire business.

## Answer Engines and video answers

What are the *'answer engines'* and where are we with them now and in the future? It's been a slow start for the answer engines like Amazon's Alexa, their issue is down to an assumption made at their outset which has turned out to be flawed.

The answer engines are only as good as the information that is fed into them. Google, Microsoft, Apple, Amazon etc. all rely on the input from the human race to build the query database. Trouble is, there are potentially 100s or 1000s of different answers to the same question. There is, therefore no perfect answer. It's easy to respond to a question that can be answered with a fact, for example, if you were to ask Alexa *"What's the weather like today?"*, it knows your location and can give you the facts from the authoritative source for that answer (the weather forecasters). There really isn't much debate over the answer so it is easy for the answer engine to reply.

Another similar example would be asking *"What's the height of Mount Everest?"*, again, no debate over the answer. Now, stop and think of some of the questions that Alexa, Bixby, Cortana, Google Home and such will struggle with, and why.

Clearly you couldn't ask *"Which political party should I support in the coming election?"* and get a satisfactory answer. You can't have a reasoned debate over politics with a machine (yet), equally you couldn't ask an opinion on anything else. Were you to ask *"what's the most reliable brand of car tyre in the world?"*, well having just searched that question on Google, the answer is apparently Michelin, followed by Bridgestone and Continental.

How do we know that is the correct answer? Perhaps I was asking from the perspective of safety and Google is defining 'reliable' as 'longest lasting'—the context is missing. Other parameters that might apply in this scenario could be:
▶ Racing
▶ Off roading
▶ Day-2-day
▶ In snow conditions
▶ Long lasting
▶ When braking

There must be 100s of different parameters and qualifying statements that you could bring into that question. There lies the rub. The answer engines struggle therefore, to understand the context in which the question is asked and therefore, cannot produce a definitive answer.

Searching the question, I asked above, there are a mere 427M results—pick the bones out of that one!

Now, the search engines are doing the job for us to an extent. I certainly don't have time to read 427M results (makes me wonder what the last result of that entire search is), but even going down the list of the first 3 pages of Google it has brought into my mind even more questions that I should be asking, before I decide which type to buy or recommend, and it is the 'recommend' issue that the answer engines are struggling with. In providing an answer they need to be certain and there clearly is no definitive answer. It's not as if I can type in (well maybe I could) the following:

*I'm a 48 year old man and I've owned in the past: a BMW which I really enjoyed driving, a Porsche which I drove really hard and used the tyres up inside 5000 miles, a Mini, a Range Rover, a Ford Transit van, a Mitsubishi truck, an Astra. My wife will use the car as much as I will. It goes on school runs as well as long distance trips at the weekend. We do some off-roading in wet conditions, we live in England and the weather is cold/wet in the winter and nice in the summer, I do about 20k miles a year, concerned about safety (not a major concern) and I don't want to pay over the top for a set of tyres, want them to last a good time... Now tell me please Google which is the best tyre for me?*

For experimental purposes I just typed that into Google. The top search result was "*Why your luxury car doesn't impress smart business women*". Now I don't know what that says about me, it's a bit worrying to be frank. Does Google think I am looking to have an affair? Quick, hide the book from the wife! Google obviously doesn't get things right all the time! I'm now chuckling imagining me asking Alexa that question and it gives an answer along those lines.

Obviously search has a long way to go, and that's before we get to being able to get answer engines to pull the correct data, personalise it and spit it out of a speaker. That is the challenge—search needs intelligence.

I recently found a page in Google's own search support forums for advertisers that backs this up, here's a screenshot:

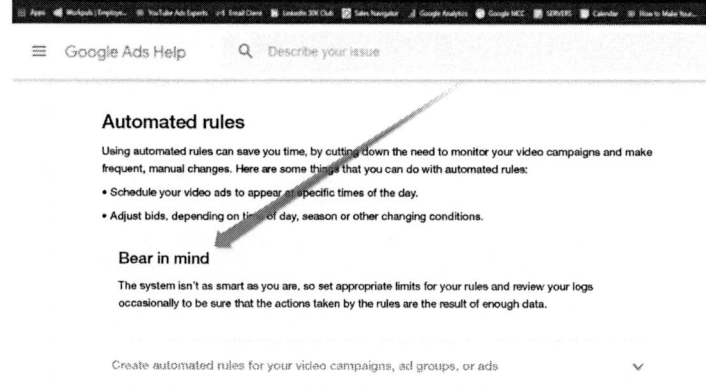

**"Bear in mind the system isn't as smart as you are"**

Well, they got that one right! 'The system' is still just that, a system. It absolutely fascinates me the way search is evolving.

Getting back to the issue at hand and talking about Answer Engines, it is clear that the next evolution in search is going to revolve around video and knowledge dissemination.

Why have the Answer Engines struggled? Because they rely on Google etc. and all the web pages that exist, the questions are not coded into those pages properly nor are the answers. Yes, we can have a 'X number of people found this answer useful' but one size does not fit all.

This is why Google is finding it easier to move to a strategy of looking for the answers and then measuring the engagement against the viewer's online profile. When I say profile, yes I mean they hold 1000s of pieces of information about all of us and our behaviour: what we buy, what we like, our political and religious beliefs, what our circle of friends looks like and much, much more, even all the dark stuff I'd imagine.

Now combine that with engagement on a video and you can learn a lot more about why the question being answered with that video matters to that particular demographic. When searching on Google in traditional text-based pages, that engagement is particularly and nearly impossible to measure accurately for the reasons discussed. Our minds wander, and we make decisions outside of the search interface. Google then struggles, but if a searcher is watching a video and they stay, they take action and watch through, we can much more easily assign a behaviour to a profile. That person would therefore, most likely like and prefer our answer were it to come out of a speaker—that makes video the clear stepping stone that the search engines require to build the Answer Engines and profile us.

Yes, they are also doing this with all social media channels, but if you want to join the dots with Google and YouTube then onto Google Home, there is pretty much only one logical conclusion. That is until true AI comes in, which is a whole other level of debate around the IOT and the fact that your fridge, kettle and washing machine may be listening to you!

## Growing your channel

It might take you months or years to achieve your goals on YouTube, so the overriding thought must be *"why do I want to grow my channel and will I enjoy doing it?"*. The second part may seem a bit odd (as the majority of this book concerns advertising), but growing your channel should be fun and if your enthusiasm comes across in your content then people will stay, they will subscribe, like, share and you will end up with a good sized audience.

Maybe you're just wanting to get your message across, maybe you want to change the world! The importance of setting your goals cannot be underestimated—know why you want to grow your channel and know who you want your audience to be. Remember, when you publish a video online, and especially on YouTube, it's there for potentially millions of people to see. Try not to think of it that way though, think as if you are talking one to one—that one viewer is extremely important—get your message right, keep people engaged and then your channel will grow consistently.

Ask yourself what questions your channel is answering for people, if you don't know why you exist on YouTube, why should anyone in your audience stay, watch, learn, view or comment?

Defining your target audience is massively important, don't just think, *'if I build it, they will come'*. That isn't going to work, and this is probably the most important part of your strategy, write down who the type of person your channel is there for, specifically.

You cannot be generic, yes there may be a temptation to say, *"my channel is for everyone"*, or *"I want everyone to watch"*, but this is where most people go wrong. When your channel is up and running and you're publishing videos and content, when people find your channel you need that person to say, *"this is the channel for me"* or think, *"I've just found exactly what I am looking for"*.

If you define the ideal subscriber for your channel, then you are one step closer to having an engaged and passionate audience. Don't make the mistake of making your channel too generic with forgettable content. If you are to do that, then your channel will not stand out and won't grow with a decent level of consistent momentum.

If you are really specific with your channel and content you will stand out, that gets rid of a lot of the competition. So, make sure you know your target audience inside out, spend time writing it down (yes write it down, it's important), what are their hobbies, what channels do they watch, how old are they, what is their education level, what's their family dynamic, what are their likes and dislikes, what are their values.

You can also ask questions such as,
- ▶ What social networks do they use?
- ▶ What devices do they own?
- ▶ What car do they drive?
- ▶ Which movies do they watch?

There are so many studies and methodologies around customer profiling or as some call it 'building a customer avatar'.

The bottom line is the more we know about a particular potential customer (in the case of your channel, your subscriber), the more likely they are to buy from you (in the case of your channel, your community member). So, in conclusion, take the time to define your audience and then drill into that audience and find out as much specific information about them as you can. The more targeted your channel is to your audience, the better it will attract and retain visitors.

You may think that by being laser focused onto your perfect subscriber, you will be excluding too many people from your potential viewership, but no, it is completely the opposite. When you focus your attention on who you are making the content for, your channel becomes far more engaging and interesting. People want to learn, fix issues, engage with other like-minded people—this is where you will create a community.

I guess what I am saying here is, steer away from becoming generic. Instead be focused, targeted and define who your target audience is, and who is that one person you are speaking to, one to one.

## Placing videos into search results

The question here we need to consider is, *"will search become more about video than text?"*. We are already seeing video preferred over text in Google, the obvious reason being that video is more engaging and can answer people's questions more quickly than text.

Google answers (the section of questions that appears on most search pages with a dropdown of multiple questions around the topic you are researching) is ever expanding, however the challenge for Google has been filling this resource.

That may seem a strange thing to say, as I can hear you perhaps saying that the answer to everything is on the internet already, but the challenge for Google has always been which answers to list (or trust). On top of that, you've got the fact that web designers have to publish their answers to questions in a specific format to be featured. As a bit of context, Google originally only listed answers from sites ranking highly already. This meant, if your site ranked on page one or two, you had a chance to also have your Q&A listed in the Google Answers section. You then had to code the answers correctly by adding 'question and answer' meta.

This limited the data and, more importantly, the quality of the content. So, Google needed a way to quickly expand the content allowing more and more Q&A into the section. We do need to ask ourselves how much this section of the Google index is used as it only soaks up a small percentage of the clicks. *BUT* the real purpose of this section of Google is to help build the resource that will support the Google Home Answer Engine in the next few years.

Google is driving hard and favouring video. If you want the best of the best SEO strategies right now, you'd be hard pushed to find any suggestion better than using video to answer your potential customer or client's questions.

Google is now able to read and understand, subtitle and derive meaning/answers and sentiment from video. When a video is ranked in search, the engagement metrics become crucial, this can only become more and more important.

In the 'good old days' of SEO, ranking for long-tail keywords was easy, and still to this day it is in some respects, apart from the fact that the highly weighted key term would most likely rank highest nowadays.

Currently the opportunity to rank video in search is enormous. The number of videos that rank is increasing all the time.

The difficult part is knowing what content to make, but as stated above the solution is obvious. Look at the answer engines, look at those questions and answers that are popping up when you search around the topic for which you want to rank your videos. There are most likely 1000's of questions.

If you choose to try and rank your videos you will need to be specific. The danger is becoming too generic, imagine for example, being given the mission to rank No.1 for the term

'Shoe' (and I realise this is a ridiculous example), but that just isn't going to happen. Possibly, with unlimited resources and a couple of years (maybe 5 or 10) it could be done, but do you have millions of pounds to spend on 'trying' to achieve with no guarantee?

The other issue you would have if you did somehow miraculously rank for the term 'Shoe', then it is far too generic a term, you're sat at the top of search for 'Shoe' and 99 out of 100 of your visitors will not find what they are looking for. At this point you lose your ranking because Google thinks 'people are not having a good experience'.

Write that down now, or get a highlighter and put a great big circle around that phrase *'people are not having a good experience'*. This is the only thing Google is concerned about—are their users finding what they want and engaging with the content (liking, sharing, watching, buying, leaving reviews, recommending, scrolling, spending time... all that good stuff), are the people voting the content up?

Now the 'Shoe' example should show you that you need to have your content MATCH EXACTLY to the expectations of the person or audience that made the search in the first place. So hopefully you can see you need to steer away from trying to please too many people, you only want the exact person that was searching for *'Shoes that protect your feet when working on a building site'*—now ask yourself, is that even specific enough?

To explain this further, while sitting here writing I have just searched that term. The answer is categorically no, however

nice it would be to be found for 'best boots or shoes to protect your feet on a building site', as it would bring orders, it is still too generic. Yes, it is a question, but can we dive deeper? Looking at the results that I've just found there are questions such as:
- What are the best shoes for construction workers?
- What are the best shoes for standing on concrete all day?
- Can you wear safety trainers on a building site?
- How can I stop my feet getting sore while wearing work boots all day?
- What is the OSHA standard for safety shoes?

In my honest opinion, we are still being too general, bearing in mind we are looking to sell boots/shoes to construction workers (as an example goal). Digging deeper there are other questions such as *"Do employers have to provide safety boots UK?"*. Then if we place ourselves in the mind of the consumer/user we can come up with other questions they might ask in this scenario, such as *"what are the safest work boots?"*. Along with:
- What are the best safety work boots?
- What are the best safety boots UK?
- What are the best work boots for standing all day?
- Are steel toe boots bad for your feet?
- Which work boots last longest?

There are clearly many considerations when choosing a work boot, however, to prove my point that the massive opportunity still exists (and if you are an SEO pro or a manufacturer of safety boots reading this then you now have your new strategy), NONE and I mean NONE of the searched answers above have been, as it stands, answered with a video answer.

How hard would it be to make a video all about safety boots—the best, the worst, featuring real construction professionals talking about their experience with different brands. You could ask them for their recommendations, how comfortable they are, are they good for the whole day, do they last years or just months or, how protective will they be? Then dive even deeper into different industries, different safety considerations, dangers, government standards, price guides, where to buy (reliable suppliers), data from tests etc.

Give more and more information, more than they could get from a short text answer and allow the consumer to make an informed decision. Suddenly I hope you can see that a video around a topic that answers all the questions the consumer would want to know ALL IN ONE PLACE is super powerful and engaging.

If promoted correctly, tagged with the right meta and then watched by the perfect audience—it WILL rank and stick. This is what Google wants.

Think of it this way, if you were in the market for a pair of hardwearing, affordable work boots, you might spend a couple of hours doing your research, you might ask a friend. You might just buy the first pair that came up, but if a video popped up addressing all of your concerns, which was presented in the right way, you are likely to watch it, and take the advice contained therein.

Google will love this content. There are just not enough businesses out there employing this as a strategy. Is it because they don't want to make the videos? No, it is mainly that they just haven't been made aware of this as a strategy or opportunity, or someone has told them that traditional SEO is the best way forward, despite it often taking months of hard work.

Then there's the good bit that I left until last.

The most surprising reward for your video content is that Google can rank it at the top of search often within a week. It is all about questions, answers, and engagement, all the things Google loves. The future is video!

Make sure you have thought through who the exact target audience for your video is, and avoid that temptation that is always there to appeal to as many people as possible (I know it goes against human nature), but this is the whole game as far as Google is concerned.

You need to be specific with the content, answer questions and get deep into the details.
- add value
- solve problems
- give support
- give statistics
- give your potential customers exactly what they need

If one video can't do it all, or you feel that temptation to become more general, make another video.

We don't all go out to make award winning YouTube channels with millions of subscribers. In many industries and niches there simply will not be the volume of ideal subscribers out there, but when your content matches your audience (your perfect audience), that is when your engagement soars. You are recommended, your videos become the answers, Google promotes your content in search and then the growth comes.

One of the biggest opportunities in search engine optimisation over the next few years, will be placing videos directly into search engine results. We are already seeing many videos pop up in search. And as a rule, all these videos appear there based on engagement rates, the metadata within the video, the title, description, links and social signals. It also depends on which websites these videos are embedded in, although now we are seeing many more videos being placed into search results by Google, directly from YouTube itself. So bear in mind it's always a great idea to link from the description of your video back to the landing page on your website as a matter of course.

There is a real skill in ranking videos. One of the obvious ways is to drive large amounts of traffic to the video which you wish to rank, however, Google needs to know the content of the video and they are getting better at doing this all the time.

Originally Google relied upon good old anchor text within the links and the video titles, tied in with the engagement rate, in order to rank a video over time. The results we do see in Google currently are still very unpredictable, someone might see their videos ranking from several years ago as they've done well and gained a lot of traction. Equally, you might see videos ranking from only a couple of weeks ago, while Google tests that particular video and the engagement rates on it. Obviously, it helps if you have a channel which is already popular and a website that ranks highly as well, but don't worry if you don't have either of those, as it is still possible to optimise videos to come to the top of the search results very quickly. That being said, there are several steps that you might have to follow in order to achieve results.

So, you want to rank a video near the top of Google, that's the result you want here. Begin by thinking about your audience and how they are going to engage with that content, remember the single most important factor that you need to take into account when trying to rank a video, will be the engagement.

- ▶ Do people stay on the video?
- ▶ Do they watch the majority of that video or do they leave halfway through?
- ▶ Do they engage in the comments?
- ▶ Do they pause or rewind the video at any point?
- ▶ Do they watch it again?

It may sound like I'm droning on here, but all of these things matter.

Start at the top with the title and make sure that it includes the keywords that you are trying to rank for, and preferably, similar keywords or phrases in the description. Ideally you have between 400 and 500 words within the description at least.

Again, keyword optimised—mentioning the phrases relevant to your audience. We can think of this as similar to the good old days of search engine ranking, although we don't want to be spammy, we do want to make sure that Google can pick up the keywords from within this section of the video description. It's a great idea here, within your description to link to other videos on similar topics that also sit within your channel, ideally you will have built up playlists around topics.

As an example, if your channel were about recipes, you might have a playlist on Indian recipes (curries), another on French recipes and another on Italian dishes and so on. For example, within your Italian playlist, you might have a sub playlist or section about pizza, one about pasta, you get the idea. Here Google will serve up (haha 'serve up'), suggested videos from your playlists if they all follow on topic and theme, then it's much easier for Google to get a feel for what you are talking about. By working in this way, you are also, hopefully, keeping the viewer on your channel for longer.

They will go on to watch more of your videos if they are on a similar theme to the one that they found or discovered in the first place, even if that first video was perhaps an advert. I can't overestimate the importance of building your channel and the playlists within it.

Next, we want to look at the content within the video itself. Yes, Google is reading that content and transcribing it into a SRT file (subtitles) and the keyword density within the video to some respect.

I'm not saying here that we deliberately spam keywords into that video, but it is always a good idea to understand that the topic you are talking about includes the keywords and similar phrases that you want to be found for.

There are very few people using this technique currently, even the videos that are showing up at the top of Google consistently, are not necessarily using this as a tactic, so I see this as an opportunity for you guys over the next few years to really optimise the content within the video.

Other good tactics involve using a great and attractive thumbnail for your video. Remember this is going to be the first thing people see on the channel, whether that be in discovery of your webpage, or in the suggested playlists as they pop up for users to consider in search. So making sure you have an attractive thumbnail rather than relying on Google to choose one for you is a great way to increase clicks through percentages onto your video.

Again, giving Google a great signal that people are finding your video more attractive than the others listed around it. That then leads into a higher position on Google, then more clicks onto promotion further up search.

Google has also recently improved its ability to read static imagery and text within videos, for example, menu items and calls to action.

So, to sum up, remember when you're placing imagery within your videos to include relevant themes and those all-important keywords. Thumbnails shouldn't be static; they should grab people's attention or 'call them to action'. Including these keywords means that Google's AI can read them and will see them as a sign of value on the topic, therefore, bettering your rank in search.

Finally, without me going into loads more detail, as I could probably write a book on the entire subject! You want people to watch your video, pause, go backwards and forwards, and find the part of the video that is most important to them, as easily as possible.

This means it's a great idea to timecode your video. Let's say you've got a video that's 10 minutes long and you're talking around a topic, again, let's use the recipe scenario. The first part of the video could just be showing which ingredients we want to use and how to combine them. Then perhaps, 7 minutes into this 10-minute video, we might be talking about how long the particular cake needs to be in the oven. It may well be that the person who had done the original search just wanted to know how long to cook a Victoria Sponge for but had done so poorly.

If in your description, you have laid out the specific sections for making this particular recipe and describe each of those parts of the video in detail, then create links in the description to each of the timestamps where all of those individual parts of the process have occurred. Then the person who was originally searching for how long they needed to cook their Victoria Sponge for, would be able to locate that section of the video immediately. This gives them the option to click on the link and go straight to the piece of information they are looking for, rather than having to watch 6 minutes of your video they didn't necessarily need or want to watch; and they will have most likely left your video in the first place. Instead, they will now be a lot more likely to stay and engage with your content, as we all know it comes down to people wanting answers as quickly as possible, so giving people the option to do just that will give them an overall better experience.

Hopefully, now you can see by adding a few simple links into your video, you are able to direct people to the part they were looking for. But more importantly from the aspect of search positioning, you have also given Google several more pieces of information that it can list in its index and measure you against.

In this example if we were trying to rank for the phrase *"how long should I cook a Victoria sponge for"*, we have now put a link directly into search that Google can spider (the term used to when Google looks for information on a piece of content) and will be able to direct folks to, knowing that the people who land on that part of your video, at that very minute, will see the exact information they were searching for.

I'm hoping I've shown you here how important it is to place the correct links within your videos and think about the description, the links and the playlists. This leads onto how you can then work with Google to get traffic to your video and then retain it.

What you don't want is traffic coming to your video that does not end up watching that content, because then Google will demote you, hurting your ability to rise up in search.

Think of it as a bit of a game, I used to be one of the top SEO people in the world (I think so at least) and some of those principles still apply to video, and it's really interesting to see Google trying to switch its strategy over to video. The only way they can do that is with your help. Fundamentally though, most people who are making video don't understand these principles; those that do are not the types of people that are really making video in the first place. A massive opportunity exists and more people need to be grabbing it with both hands!

## Ranking Videos and the new world of SEO (search engine optimisation)

What's the only thing that can put Google out of business? Probably nothing, however, the only threats that Google sees are the 'answer engines' such as Alexa, Cortana, Bixby, Siri etc.

Put yourself in Google's shoes and imagine a world perhaps 10 years from now, where we are all searching using our voices and asking questions. That's suddenly become a massive issue for Google, then nobody is reliant, as we are today, on Google search. Google then doesn't enjoy the monopoly it has today and it is one of multiple 'answer engines'.

The race is on. All are racing to be the answer engine of choice and help us all not only search but automate tasks within the home, solve problems, playback music, create our shopping lists etc. Depending on your point of view you might decide that Alexa or Siri or perhaps Cortana is winning in the race to become the dominant player in the voice search space. Google has Google Home or Google Nest, my personal opinion is they need to give it a personality, but the current mode of operation allows the owner of the device to change the name of the device in the app, but Google still only allows you to wake the device up with "Hey Google" or a similar command. Hey, what do I know, there will be some massive brains and focus groups, research etc. having been applied to this. I still think they are wrong. More to the point though, which device actually wins will depend on the answers it can give and how useful it ultimately is. Why that is important and how this ties into the use of video is very interesting and important.

Currently we are stuck with text-based searches, Google traditional search. This is because the answer engines just aren't up to it, they spew out rubbish or just facts. The answers given are standard at best. So, how does Google still hold all the cards? Google is using YouTube as the answer, it's clear that the main use of YouTube other than entertainment is to answer people's questions, in video form. Google LOVES this because it allows them to serve videos to a wide range of people and gauge their reaction, in terms of watch time, engagement, clicks—all manner of differing behaviour tracking can be measured. This is really important because when you look at who to serve which answer to through a speaker which only has a voice instruction, it needs to know a lot more about who is being provided with that answer. As well as with all search engines (and this will be true for the answer engines as well), people will continue to search using them provided they can find what they want quickly and trust the provided information. Google is actively using YouTube as the test bed for video content and massively favouring video content because of this. Take it one step further along this journey into the future and you'll then understand the following :

- Google doesn't experiment with listings on the first page in main search, the algorithm ranks trusted content and serves it up knowing that those websites are the ones consumers of the information trust, based on engagement.
- YouTube does not follow the same rules, publishers can expect their videos to rank very quickly (sometimes in under an hour). Imagine if you could rank your web page in Google search in an hour that would be amazing? But that IS what is possible on YouTube. The reason being that Google wants to actively test video content and its quality plus engagement rates.
- Videos ranked on YouTube that are found by the algorithm to be of sufficient quality and engagement are promoted to main Google search, as Google favours video so much now because it wants to understand how we interact with questions and the answers provided in video form.

The way different people and groups interact with video will determine how answers are served up in voice search in the future—hence video is the bridge from text-based search to voice-based search. Text-based SEO will therefore be quickly superseded by video SEO and ranking videos on YouTube should be the No.1 go-to tactic when starting any SEO campaign from now on, FACT. ∎

# ▶ Technical shit and the boring chapter (nerdom) | Simon

## Some of the basics of YouTube Ads

▶ Firstly, let's look at some of the potential pitfalls you could find yourself in; things that might cause your campaigns to stall or underperform.

The number one GOLDEN RULE that is going to save you a boatload of time and is the cause of failure when beginning working on YouTube (and many other online digital marketing campaigns) is perfectionism! I've worked with 100s of clients and this is always a barrier that we have to overcome. It delays the whole process as a rule, causing inaction.

As a rule, if you can get your ads made and then stick to a formula, you can then get to a point where you are able to test these ads. Testing and learning is what we want most from our campaigns, then we can produce what will end up as the 'perfect campaign'.

If you feel yourself getting precious about every little detail, stop. You can take your time making that perfect ad, but it will no doubt delay the process and, therefore the final results if you procrastinate—there is no such thing as the perfect ad! Yes, it may be perfect for one person (and remember, that person is usually you), but producing an advert that is tailored for your entire audience is practically impossible. We need something that works and can be improved upon over time.

**Step one** in YouTube campaign creation is to set realistic and achievable goals to work towards. I'll talk about patience later, but it's important to set your goals and the parameters that you are going to work within. Why? Because success comes from following the data, not hope!

If you are going to say to yourself at any point during the campaign *"it will be better next time I run this ad"* and the data doesn't support that, you are going to go down a rabbit hole and continually put your judgement ahead of the data, wasting more time and your budget.

Here's a good analogy and way to frame YouTube Advertising in your mind. Treat the process like a game of cards:

*'Imagine you're playing poker'*

The next question is, 'Am I playing with my own money, or is someone else backing me?'

The reason I want you to think of it in that way is because you need to decide from the outset how much you are willing to lose. That sounds awful coming from someone who's passionate about the opportunities on YouTube, but this is one of the limiting factors that will kill your campaigns before they get going.

Back to the poker table, there's always a table stake, the amount you have to *'pay to play'* or an amount you are willing to risk.

Now, in poker there are many, many different levels, you can play at the £5 tables, you can play at the £1000 tables. Here though Google is the dealer, and they want their *'entry fee'*. The difference with Google is you can win nearly all the time with patience (there's that word again), oh, and that's another card game that you can win most of the time! Yet here we are concerning ourselves with poker, the big boys' and girls' game.

As a good rule of thumb, I'd encourage you to get into the mindset where you are always risking your own money. If you're an agency running ads for a client, the worst that can happen is you lose a client if things don't go well. Lose the client and you lose some of your income, so effectively you are always playing the game with your own money.

There is a reason I use the poker analogy and it's because Google Ads and YouTube Ads are practically a game. There are a set of rules, there are other players you are up against, you have a bankroll and you're always trying to move to the next table up by increasing your daily budgets and achieving more and more wins. At the core of what I do is *'the game'*, I'm still learning every day, as are our staff. It's the enjoyment of that and the winning that keeps me interested and gives me the love of what I do.

So, now we are *'in the game'* let's talk about budgets, what are you prepared to lose I think was how I phrased it. Now, when pitching to clients I wouldn't start by asking, "*So Mr Client, how much would you like to risk or lose on this campaign*" that would be funny. Perhaps I should try that in a meeting and see the reactions (who knows it might break the ice and get a decent debate going).

The point I am trying to make is that we need a testing budget to begin with, there needs to be a period over which that budget is spread, and the client expectations need to be managed through the testing phase. This is not a 'plug and play' solution. Yes, a level of success will be achievable within the test phase (usually the first couple of months), but all too often clients come with the expectation that 24 hours after their campaign has gone live, sales will begin flowing, there is a lovely juicy ROI, everyone is running around high fiving each other, we are all millionaires in the making. If that were the case, I would be a wizard and also a billionaire, having launched many of my own products and sold zillions of pounds simply by starting with a £5 a day budget and ending up spending £5M a day after 3 months! It just doesn't work like that.

So, setting expectations and goals becomes extremely important from the outset. REALISTIC expectations!

Writing that word reminds me of a campaign that we undertook, where in the onboarding process, the client was asked how many registrations for his webinar he expected from his £2,000 budget for the first month. The reply nearly made me fall off my chair, but now I'm older and wiser, I knew where the actual expectations should be set. The client had said "*Well, I think we should be able to get registrations for roughly 20-30p each, so 8 to 10,000?*". This wasn't, by the way, a webinar by a famous teen pop star who's got millions of followers (in which case it would have been super easy to achieve those numbers), this was an insurance product in the property market! Yes, we love working on those types of accounts too, I'd suspect the creative department doesn't love them quite as much, however, remember that for me, it is all about the numbers. The numbers don't lie. I explained how the process worked and went into detail about the audience, click-through rates, awareness projections and on-site conversion percentages (another expectation you often need to manage as clients can be known to 'exaggerate the truth'). Let's say we came to a figure of between £3 and £4 a registration for this particular client—once the campaign matures.

Note my '*once the campaign matures*' caveat, that is where I am telling the client in no ambiguous terms that the first month or two is a '*learning and testing*' phase. This is where Google wants to see if you are serious and want to play the game, the single biggest mistake people make when entering these campaigns is a lack of patience. If we were sat at the poker table, you'd be an idiot to go '*all-in*' on the first hand of the game. You might win, but that would be luck and forgive me if I seem a little blunt, no client is going to accept an excuse of "*we were unlucky, bad luck old chum*".

Now I'm sat here typing away with a big smile on my face thinking about a couple of past clients that I'd have loved to say that to when they had massively (in their own minds) over egged the expectations from a campaign.

We as ads professionals do have to put ourselves in the clients mind though. It's extremely easy to give the impression that a campaign will yield amazing results, that it is the '*campaign delivery method you have been seeking for so long and the answer to all your businesses problems*', I suppose. I guess the answer is to not '*oversell*' the service, but again, manage the expectations of the client properly and make sure they are clear on the direction they want, yielding results, from day one.

More often than not it is experience that pays off. That experience and insight is backed up by the data, and great data leads to great insight. Insight leads to good decisions, testing confirms your hypothesis, planning and strategy, whilst following the system leads to predictable results. When it becomes predictable you can scale campaigns—and at that point, there is no luck involved.

The AI has to learn, and as Google says itself, *'the system is not as smart as you are'* so 'luckily' for us, humans are still required and should realistically always be required. The Google systems are making it easier and easier for everyday advertisers to use the tools and get their adverts out there in front of millions, and, of course, get results. It is those that plan properly, use the data, test/learn and don't gamble with their budgets that will win out.

This is an end to step 1, patience. Set up your first campaigns with a budget that you are prepared to lose if nothing goes to plan, and don't always expect fireworks from day one. There is no 'magic secret', it's all in the testing.

Now, let's get into the term 'patience', don't mistake patience for lack of action.

**Step 2** Another campaign killer is TINKERING. Tinkering comes as a result of impatience, wanting to 'make things happen'. This is a killer! Making continuous adjustments to your campaigns will be a massive temptation, and you may think you are improving things. You are absolutely not. What you are doing however, is causing confusion by sending more and more varying signals to Google, saying that you are *'not happy'* with how the campaign is set up. Google can take 7 to 14 days to learn and decide on placements of your ads based on the settings. Think of it this way, you put your campaign live and two days later there is nothing happening, or it is spending money and there are no conversions.

If at this point you make adjustments, we can think of Google as a game of snakes and ladders, square 2 and you've just hit the *'restart the game'* button.

Google says to itself, OK, go back to square one and start the game again. Sometimes you do need to be brave and trust your instincts and trust the data you have from previous campaigns. Despite that, as a rule (and chisel this one into your desk if you are going to be running big budgets on Google), DO NOT TINKER WITH CAMPAIGNS.

What we have just said about 'tinkering' is completely opposite to what we think we should be doing. We naturally want to *'take action'* and work hard for clients. We are conditioned to think that action equals results. With Google there is no secret recipe, no silver bullet, no luck. If you follow the rules and don't expect instant gratification, then you will succeed.

Trust me, where YouTube Ads are concerned you need patience, you need to trust the system and let the campaigns learn—everything comes to those who wait. The problem is that most people can't afford to wait or think it is a magic formula, patience wears thin and they probably turn their campaigns off just before they are about to catch and grow. Like the greatest poker players, the best ads people let these campaigns learn, they watch closely but don't give away any signals (tinkering) and they take their time to move past the early mistakes.

I am here to tell you that focus is everything—focus on the goals you've set for your campaign at the outset. Don't *just try a few things that you've heard on the net that could be good ways to go*', stick to your plan. That means you must have a clear plan in the first place with expectations and numbers that you think are realistic to hit. Then and only then, can you judge your results against the plan. Analysing reasons for failure is just as important as what worked. Here is one of the best pieces of advice you will get from our book, it seems very simple, but it is easily overlooked.

**Make notes, lots of them.**

If you are running campaigns on Google it does provide a 'change history', in which you can see all the changes you made to individual campaigns. I've seen lots of PPC pros rely on this change history so that they can refer back. I've been guilty of this myself in the past, but the issue with the '*changes history'* section of Google, is that it doesn't answer the '*why'* you made the particular adjustment, be that a change in budget, audience, demographic or so on. The single most important thing we are trying to learn is the 'why'?

What was the reasoning that led to that change? (again without tinkering) Yes, it is so incredibly tempting to make changes for the sake of changes or *'because it feels right'*, but, stick to the plan.

Does your reasoning match the campaign objective and how long are you going to wait to see if those learnings made the difference that you were expecting? So, your notes should include a snapshot of where you are 'right now' against the campaign objectives, your observations, reason for change, change made, time to learn (how long you will leave this before next change), age of campaign and lastly expected result. My campaign adjustment template is below:

**Filed against the client name and campaign**
*Date:*
*Campaign name:*
*Ad Group name:*
*Creative: (What is the content, style, type, reasoning):*
*Daily budget for this campaign/ad group: £ / £*
*Time ads live (number of days this ad has run):*
*Iteration (has a similar campaign run before and if so, how many times):*
*Objective (what is the overall desired outcome):*
*Time since the last adjustment (days):*
*Observations since last change (why and what are we changing):*
*Date next adjustment allowed:*
*Spend max to next adjustment:*
*Were last adjustments successful (if not, why not, what was unexpected?):*
*Adjustment being made now and why:*
*Expected results from this change:*

If you can stick to making your notes, over the period of the campaign you can learn, and it is the surprises that will make your day and amaze you. We all have a predisposition to guess what will work. Have an open mind, trust me you will be constantly amazed at where the results come from.

Getting too dialled in at the start of a campaign is also an issue (and temptation)—you have to make a judgement at some point, yes you may well want to start with the 'perfect audience' but do that at your own peril. Your campaigns may not run, or you end up paying over the odds for the conversions and impressions. The real issue though is if you make assumptions without letting the data tell you, you risk missing out on potential audiences that could have delivered amazing results.

As a quick example on a very basic level, we were running a campaign for a cycling holidays business. Immediate (and sensible) assumption would be to go after people interested in cycling, well obviously, and members of cycling clubs, again obvious.

That gave a decent audience size and somewhere to start. The temptation then, was to overlay these audiences with people who were *'in the market'* or actively searching for a cycling holiday. At which point we had created the perfect audience (or you would have thought). However, by over-laying the intent this then cut an audience from the hundreds of thousands to only a few hundred people. The audience was then not big enough to serve or we had to bid up the cost per view to make it trigger, making it potentially not viable within the client's budget.

How did we solve the dilemma—get brand awareness along with conversions? Taking the 'cycling' and 'cycling club' audience was easy, we knew that the in-market audience was too small, so we looked deeper into the customer profile of the people who actually went on cycling holidays and why. Which newspapers they read, how old they were, what food they like etc.

The business we were promoting was offering something outside of the norm, something involving more of an experience including great food. The target was not the man or woman who wanted a sporty/exercise-based lifestyle holiday, we were clearly after a more well-off and older audience. See what I did there? I made a massive assumption, wrong!

The key was to write all these assumptions down, then test them, because if we didn't test then we didn't have the data to prove the assumption (or disprove it as things turned out). The data that came back was not that the older audience would want this experience, yes, they did, but they didn't want to combine that with a cycling holiday. Finding out these pieces of golden insight helped the business owner completely understand and transform his business and marketing strategy going forward.

Hopefully you can see that had we not tested the audiences properly and without producing the negative test (but still targeted of course), the campaign would have failed (or produced very average results). These simple tests at the outset need to be looked at as investments, that one piece of information is potentially worth hundreds of thousands of pounds to that business from a very small test. Equally, had we concentrated on the 'perfect audience' we could have learned very little and purely confirmed in the mind of the business owner what he already knew. Where is the added value in that for him?

Getting clients excited about this level of data is really important, the value is then seen, and great partnerships are formed, that is what great marketing looks like. Not *'we run your ads'.* Those agencies that don't feed back and document results properly are effectively stealing some of the client's IP. What happens if an agency runs campaigns in a siloed manner for a client and has success, but then over time they either get lazy (as is a problem in the agency world, but that is a whole chapter in its own right), then the client decides that they need a new agency and more help (or just to reinvent their marketing). The incumbent agency is sacked, that agency walks away with all the data and learnings, the new agency if lucky gets access to a level of insight, BUT they are often starting with a clean slate, nobody is the winner there.

The cycle starts over and the agency/client wheel turns. This is where the whole agency world needs a shake-up. If you are a client reading this, sort your agency out, get them reporting properly, giving you all of the data they have. There should be a completely transparent and open relationship.

I recently sacked a client as he wouldn't tell me who was running his Facebook Advertising, as they had an *'undisclosed system'.* All I wanted to do was collaborate with them for the good of the client. When the client eventually did bend to my way of thinking, the other agency refused to collaborate (in case I saw what he was doing and his *'secret sauce'*), and the client was dropped by us.

It turned out that the Facebook Ads agency were running remarketing to our YouTube Ads. The point I am scrabbling around to make here is, marketing needs to be absolutely collaborative, it should always have the client or campaign results at its heart as a common goal. Beware of the agency who doesn't share their reasoning or their tactics, as they have your business data and if they leave with that data and insight, they are effectively stealing your business, and potentially, taking it to a competitor.

The danger is thinking there is a *'secret sauce'*. All day long I see various adverts from so-called gurus proclaiming they have a *'system'* that has built millions of pounds of business for their clients.

The bottom line is that if these 'gurus' were indeed able to make miracles happen, so many clients would have flocked to them that they would not be needing to sell their system. If the *'system'* is that good, why sell it?

The truth of the matter is that these so called gurus are either afraid of hard work (they don't actually want to help clients by working for them), OR worse still, they are actually akin to *'snake oil salesmen'* selling an off the shelf method (that does have some value), but they themselves have discovered that selling a system is better than actually working.

Yet ask yourself, if they are that good then why are they selling the tools that got them there? Frankly I'm fed up with this culture that has sprung up online, wrapping something up in a shiny package and bragging about it. There is no stopping Facebook promoting these businesses though, as typically Facebook is taking 50% of the revenue generated. The advertiser sticks in 100K, gets back 200K and both win. Well everyone except the unsuspecting buyer.

The learning here is, and this is not just in relation to YouTube or Facebook advertising, there really is no substitute for hard work, the secret sauce doesn't exist. If there is something in it you'll not beat those of us that know the real game and have the experience to apply the knowledge learned from the data.

Don't get caught in the trap of thinking there is a magic bullet and your ads will deliver easily, from day one, with very little effort. It's hard, it's a long road but there is gold at the end of it, for those that work hard.

Moving on from the 'magic bullet', the other thing you need to make sure you do is, avoid 'giving things a go'. There are so many people talking about advertising and the various techniques and latest best practices and it is extremely tempting to give some of these things you are bombarded with 'a go'.

That is usually a recipe for losing focus, losing money and ultimately, getting disheartened and giving up. The only thing you need to trust is the data you have from your own learnings and campaign statistics, your notes and reasoning behind the changes you made, and why.

Google wants us to all rely on their 'smart campaigns' and optimisation settings, they are in the game too. Let's not beat around the bush or sugar coat things, they are in the game of taking your budget, consistently.

We need to be smarter than that.

I've said it more than once in this book, Google itself says *"remember the system is not as smart as you are"*, but Google will tempt you to use all the shiny, smart bidding tools and automated conversions, inviting you to be lazy and to think they know best.

Always remember their goal is to get you to spend as much as possible. Fact.

You'd not trust your pension money to an amateur or someone who said they *'have bought and sold a few shares'* in their time. You'd want an expert, a day trader with a record of producing consistent returns—that is the difference between someone who knows a little bit about Google's tools and someone who's used the system for 20 years. As in all things, a little knowledge is a very dangerous thing. I know how to build a wall (I can buy some bricks, cement, a spirit level, etc), but the chances of me doing the job right are slim, plus I'd take 10 times longer than a pro who has the experience. Yes, it is going to cost me more to employ a pro but it will be done right and quickly, with a guarantee that it will not fall down!

## What should your initial goals be for your campaigns?

**Step 1:** We always talk about getting your campaigns to *'wash their face'* in the first instance, meaning that it should pay for itself, cover costs and inspire confidence going forward. That is a long way from the 'silver bullet' of 8 or 10× ROI many people sell as a utopian dream for month 1, or where you hope your campaigns will end up with significant ROI.

In the first couple of months of running your campaigns your initial goals therefore, should be to cover your costs, achieve that and you've got the building blocks for success. In quite a few client examples it will take longer and can require significant investment (depending on your product, market, audience, competition etc.).

**Step 2:** Get to a positive ROI, media spend is less than profit achieved from the activity. Note that I'm not talking about ROAS (return on ads spend), as that calculation although it has some value (spend vs return) it can be an indication of the way a campaign is going. We would much rather track profitability of the campaign than an X vs Y ROAS. If you're working with a product that has 20% margin it's obviously far more difficult to achieve a profitability than if your product has 50% gross margin, but in both the examples if you spent £1000 on ads and received £5000 back you'd have the same ROAS, in this example, 5×. One campaign would have returned £1000 profit and broken even, the other would have returned £2,500 and clearly is far more successful. So, stick to calculations based on profit, not ROAS.

**Step 3:** Refine your campaigns, learn more and scale your spend up. Once you have a positive ROI which is consistent, you can scale quickly and grow your returns. This is where we can learn more and drive more insight about the audiences, bring in some automated elements, and make more profits to reinvest.

Once you reach the point of consistently achieving a good return on investment then it becomes all about the testing, reiteration and learning. This really is the fun part but also dangerous. As a general rule don't follow the suggestions Google makes unless you have a few hundred conversions (valuable conversions of good quality).

In a recent example of scaling incorrectly, we worked with a client who, in the past, had a very large number of conversions in their account (in the thousands) and had a Google Ads account with a historical spend in excess of £100K.

The business owners neglected to tell us that the majority of these previous sales were from a less than ideal type of customer. That information came out very quickly during the discovery phase of our campaigns. The lesson being, it's more about quality of conversion once you reach the campaign optimisation stages. Often it is that additional level of insight that is required. By simply changing the AOV (average order value) and putting in a minimum we cleaned out the sub-optimal customers and built a new set of goals around lifetime customer value rather than short term gains where they had been historically.

## Letting Google Learn

OK I know I keep saying it, but patience really is the key. I've seen campaigns take days to learn, others over a month, some 2 to 3 months. Can you speed things up though? The answer to that is yes, but that comes with an element of additional risk.

If we can consistently teach Google what we are looking to achieve then it will respond, the trick though is to understand that there are possibly lots of different conversion events that we can show as having value.

Obviously, the most important conversion we are aiming for is a sale or customer acquisition. However, from the beginning of a campaign, the numbers of these 'ideal' conversions could be low, so we can encourage Google with other conversion events that we know eventually lead to the ideal conversions. When beginning a campaign, you may find you need to use Google's *'maximise conversions'* goal setting. This is not ideal, but it will spend your budget and begin the process of understanding where your conversions are coming from.

As an example, you might have a form fill as your conversion goal or a phone call, brochure download, add to cart etc. The actual goal is customer acquisition, sale or enquiry, but the issue which you will face in the learning phase, is that we may struggle to get these golden conversions in the early stages of campaigns.

Therefore, we need to actively leverage the lesser value and more common value conversions in the early stages of campaigns (as there are lots more of these available). We need to teach Google as quickly as possible, and if you set the only conversion that you are tracking as the *'golden conversion'* at the outset, Google will take far longer to reach that 100-conversion target where you are then able to move over to a CPA or TCPA model for your campaign.

Think of it this way, you are using the lesser conversion metrics to teach Google we need more of these to achieve the final conversion. Once the campaign learns how to generate X then we know that for every 10X we get Y, therefore we can use X as a stepping stone in the journey toward where we need to be. Without that bridge your job is a lot harder, takes longer and costs far more of your testing budget.

## The Importance of Tracking

I literally cannot stress enough the importance of tracking your ads properly—I've said it a few times in the book and it's the number one piece of the puzzle. The whole algorithm and AI that Google is using will use the tracking and conversion data as its backbone and foundation. You want it on every single webpage, inside your apps, on your socials, everywhere. The more you can track, the more you can feed Google. Google and Facebook are even recording and monitoring the words that you speak. Even our devices, phones, Alexa, Siri, even your toaster or your fridge, they are all listening and tracking everywhere you go (well maybe not the fridge, he's just chilling, but eventually he'll be telling Jeff when you need some more milk or how balanced a diet you are eating).

The Intelligence that's been built up behind the Google algorithm really is absolutely amazing. They will get this to the point where they know what you want before you know what you want. One of the famous scenes that I do often talk about is the scene from Minority Report, where Tom Cruise is walking through the airport and all of the ads that are popping up on the screens around him are completely personalized to him and him only. That's already happening today, so where will we be in 10 years time? There's no getting away from it, unless you want to go and live in the woods in a bunker, wait, there are actually people that do that right?

Tracking and letting Google's algorithm know that you've had success is the one thing that really, really, matters. You either bury your head in the sand and burn your ads budget or get with the program and let Google learn. So, I guess what I am saying is that there are no half-arsed measures that will get you through, it's all or nothing and if you aren't prepared to learn and put all the tracking into your campaigns, go get a decent agency that knows what they are doing. There are several different types of campaign that you can run. A couple of the most popular would be 'maximise conversions' and 'cost-per-acquisition', others such as 'cost per click', 'awareness' or 'discovery' etc. exist but let's just concentrate for a start on the cost per acquisition campaign type.

Circling back to teaching Google, when you're going to run a cost per acquisition campaign Google needs to learn. It needs to learn what a conversion looks like and the type of person that's delivered that conversion. When we're setting up campaigns on Google, we often find that if you start with a customer acquisition campaign, which a lot of people do, this is where the mistakes happen.

The issue is that if you start with a customer acquisition campaign based on a fixed CPA (cost per acquisition) and you have just started, you therefore have little or no acquisition data. Google is really a little bit lost to start with because you've set a TCPA (target cost per acquisition) and all you have done is said to Google—'try your best to do this for me'. Yes Google may say something like 'other advertisers like you have set a cost per acquisition of £X' but that really isn't helpful IMHO.

This is where the campaign choice 'maximise conversions' comes in. If you set up a maximise conversions campaign it will spend your money, it will spend the entirety of your budget, trying to find you conversions. You're gambling at this point (remember earlier I told you to make notes and plan), well this is where you really want to pay attention to your campaigns. The purpose of the maximise conversions campaign setting, is to tell Google to *'go and get me as many conversions as you can, spend all my budget and tell me if I did a good job with the targeting'*. Don't be surprised if Google spends all your budget and there are very few conversions (sometimes none), that then makes advertisers feel like there were no conversions available. What Google then expects you to do is make changes and learn, if you don't do that you may as well throw the money out the window as you're back to square one. If you're an advertiser and your agency turned around to you and said 'we need to spend the entirety of your budget just on the testing phase with no guarantee of any results', that might sound like they had gone completely mad. By accepting the 'maximise conversions' setting on Google that's exactly what you are signing up for, and it may sound quite daunting, but in the long run if we let Google learn, we can drive down the cost per acquisition. The issue with all these types of campaigns is gaining enough data to make good decisions—that takes investment at the outset, for Google and you to learn. Too often people think that switching on a campaign means it's optimised from day one and the orders will flow in, nope!

You should consider a minimum budget of at least $50/£50 per day to get going and get data coming in, if you're not comfortable spending a test budget then get a decent agency involved. In terms of a launch campaign that would equate to roughly $1,500 to £1,500 a month and at least a 3-month commitment. So within the first month you would expect to learn and let Google learn what conversions look like. Once you've achieved roughly 100 conversions into your campaigns then it's quite easy to switch it over to a cost per acquisition model.

My suggestion would be to start at roughly £15 or $15 for your target TCPA, depending on your offer and see where your campaign goes. It's always a good exercise to ask yourself what an acceptable cost of customer acquisition is and work backwards. As an example, you might accept £50 as a cost to acquire a new customer. If that's the case and you convert one in three enquiries into an order, then £17-£18 would be your target cost of enquiry if you follow.

Obviously, in some industries the cost to acquire a customer is way beyond that, but with YouTube advertising I believe it to be the lowest CPA for qualified leads or customers of any of the social channels, just because you can get traffic to your site, who's viewed your video and engaged. This results in higher levels of trust, higher on-site conversion stats and much lower cost per click than traditional PPC search ads. I've seen clients that had acquisition costs in the thousands (all be it for services that cost hundreds of thousands) reduce their cost to acquire a new customer by 10× just by switching over to a YouTube-First approach.

Once you have the 50-100 conversions you need to switch to target cost of acquisition. The best strategy is to begin with a TCPA of 2× your acceptable acquisition cost (that may sound odd). Well what we need to do is give Google a bit of wiggle room in the first instance, let's not put the straight-jacket on straight away, you'll find anyway that if your bid is for example £25 per enquiry, you should see CPA below that. Your daily budget needs to be 3-4× your CPA as a minimum as well, so in that example you would need a daily budget of £100+.

Then you need to go on and see if your campaign can deliver any impressions at all—this would allow you as the advertiser to decide, or have a good idea, as to where the campaign might end up. It's here that things can get super confusing. If you start getting impressions at this sort of level, you will most certainly be able to drive the cost per acquisition down below £15. There's quite a lot talked around this figure as a starting point. If your campaign does not deliver anything in the first 3 to 5 days (and this is a minimum period to let Google learn, preferably you would let it learn over the first 4 weeks), a massive opportunity to make a mistake exists at this testing point as many advertisers presume that they will get results from the moment their campaigns go live. If your campaign delivers nothing in the first 3 to 5 days with a target cost per acquisition of £15, you could then just add £5 to the TCPA, for example, and then see in the next 3 to 5 days if it delivers some results. Better to do this and slowly creep the budget upward, rather than dive in too high in the first instance.

Slowly increment. What you need to think about is what other advertisers are bidding to get the traffic that you're after? Is your target market particularly competitive? Is the product that you're selling a high margin product and therefore something that people are prepared to bid highly on?

Equally, be realistic—don't expect your ads to run in a competitive market for a really low target cost per acquisition. Work with the figures that you think are honest and acceptable, and see where that gets you to (after the testing phase). Remember that the testing is the investment, and advertising is not free. Don't get me wrong, there is plenty of space out there on YouTube and it's still relatively untouched by most industries. It may just be a case of letting your campaign learn for a few more days. This is where it's important to be really patient. Again I cannot stress enough how important it is to be patient when your campaigns are running and learning—please resist the temptation to be a 'Tinkering Timmy', nobody likes him, he fiddles with stuff and it always ends up in a mess, but it's never his fault.

There is of course the 'suggested TCPA' that Google will put in front of you when you're building your campaigns. It will often say 'other advertisers are bidding between X and Y' and so it tries to encourage you to bid higher than you necessarily might have wanted to do. As with a lot of the Google products, I'm here to tell you that you don't necessarily have to bid in line with their suggested bid, it's always better to start much lower and then try to find the bottom point, working your way up. You'll often find that this is a lot lower than the original lowest bid range that Google offers you—why is that the case Google?

## Building exclusion lists

One thing that you'll find extremely useful when running YouTube campaigns (this applies to display as well) is to build yourself a continuously growing list of exclusions. For example, treat the channels/videos/placements/websites as the equivalent of 'negative keywords', the places where you don't want your adverts to appear.

Within the Adwords interface you'll find a menu item that says, "*See where your ads showed*"—this gives you the full list of all the places Google chose to display your ads. In the case of YouTube campaigns it can also show you the list of channels and videos in which your video adverts were shown.

The great thing with YouTube in particular is that you are only charged for a TrueView—a view that lasts at least 30 seconds long for Instream adverts. Obviously there are other ad formats that are charged by impression (mainly where you are not allowing the viewer to skip). Below the *'where your ads showed'* is an exclusion tab, so you can pick from the placements that are not performing, add them to the exclusions lists and tell Google to not use that channel/video again. Equally where the display network or app store is being used then you are able to exclude those placements as well.

It's a really good idea to build and save lists to use across multiple campaigns or exclude from an entire account. You may also want to have specific lists that you apply against specific ad groups.

To demonstrate, let's imagine we are advertising a financial product such as loans or mortgages to people who are parents in their mid-thirties, who have children (some basic targeting).

When targeting people who have kids, the issue can be that their devices are often being used by their children as well, it's therefore not hard to imagine that a home PC may be being used by a child early in the evening, for watching YouTube videos or playing games. The device being primarily used by the parent, may trigger your advert to trigger into a channel being watched by the young person who's not your target audience.

So, we need to look at the placements that are appearing in the *'where my ads showed'* section. Let's say we see *'Minecraft videos'* or anything else that is clearly not the parent watching, this gives us a start on our exclusions list. Building these lists over time will allow you to then have saved lists that make it easy to kick off new campaigns with an immediate improvement to the targeting from day one, ultimately saving budget.

As a side note while talking about exclusions, be careful that your adverts aren't straying into music videos. It's one of the places on YouTube that doesn't lend well to conversions (unless you deliberately want to target those of particular music genres or a product that is going after these specific audiences). The reason it can be a good idea to exclude music as a placement, is that the person who's using YouTube for music, is generally only listening and not watching (again you can be building exclusions, there are general settings to help prevent your ads straying into music videos). Instead treat YouTube as lean-in advertising, meaning you want your audience's full attention.

TVs and tablets (device targeting) are not always great marks for placement when you're looking for a sale or lead conversion. These can of course be excluded at campaign level. Combine these with your exclusion lists and you're halfway there to a good jumping off point for a new campaign.

While we are talking about exclusions, you can add multiple placements. If you download the entire list of where your ads have shown, you can manipulate the data and set criteria for the exclusions you want to apply. You can then take that list and re-upload it into the multiple exclusions tabs. Each of these lists can contain up to 5,000 exclusions, and you can effectively exclude 10s of thousands of unwanted or underperforming placements.

*Note*—be careful to not exclude a placement until you've tested it.

## It's not all about ROAS or the initial profitability

Some of the very best campaigns we have seen are all based around '*lifetime value*' of the customer. If you have the ability to build a campaign that pays for itself at the front end (i.e. it is not losing you money or only costing a minimal amount), then you are into a far more powerful strategy than trying to achieve all your profits from your media spend.

Remember, Google/Facebook etc. all want their slice of the turnover. As a rule, and looking at Amazon and eBay, those businesses operate by roughly wanting to earn 15-20% of your turnover. That is where they see the sweet spot.

Imagine a scenario where it costs you £25 to acquire a customer and the profit on your initial sale to that customer is £15, you're losing £10 per new customer right? What's the lifetime value of the customer though? If we know that now we can sell regularly to that same customer. The lifetime value could be 100s or 1000s of pounds. Now we have a campaign that will possibly dominate our market and bring in a consistent flow of new business, which will, inevitably, compound over the next few months and years. So make sure you have built LTV (lifetime value) into all your campaign models.

Google and Facebook etc. may have had their slice of the initial acquisition, but if you've built a full nurture, remarketing and customer relationship management system on the back end, they aren't getting their hands on the profits generated there!

This is where, in the long term, all businesses that trade online need to go, as none of us can consistently afford to give away 20% of our turnover to the advertisers and agencies (unless of course they are feeding us customers with good LTV). ∎

## ⏭ An introduction to how to approach YouTube Ads | Simon

▶ There are several different options, so let's take a look at the main routes to gaining traction. Obviously there are SO many options available it would be impossible to cover them all in a book like this, so, I'm going to take you through some of the basics.

**Some YouTube Advert Formats to choose from.**

There's a large variety of YouTube advertising options to drive various campaign objectives. These include:

**Display adverts (discovery campaigns):** These are great for brand awareness, but more difficult to get clicks to a target website, as CTA doesn't include a click option. These types of ads appear on the right hand side of the suggested videos, next to the video being featured (on the desktop platform only). (Be careful not to let Google automatically expand the targeting into the entire display network, as there are lots of bots operating there).

**Overlay adverts:** These translucent overlay ads which, as a rule appear on the lower 20% of your video while playing. Text and images can be used with nice opportunities for CTA.

**Skippable video adverts 'In-Stream':** Currently the most widely used and exploited type of YouTube adverts. Here your adverts come in and interrupt the viewers experience (it can be a great tactic to use a pattern interrupt here or show a viewer something similar, but more exciting than what they were watching). There are ads you see before, during, or after a video, which a viewer can skip after 5 seconds. As a rule, you only pay if someone watches 30 seconds or more, so those people who skip during the first 29 seconds count as an impression and you're not charged. If they take action and click through to your site you'll be charged, hopefully having learned more than they would have done had they been exposed to a traditional text based, PPC advertising campaign.

**Non-skippable video adverts:** It's possible to *'force'* the viewer to watch part of your advert. The non-skippable adverts will always be chargeable, and you've got 6 seconds before the viewer can skip. The goal here is to capture attention very quickly and keep the viewer watching. There's no limit to the length of advert you can show, so why not have an advert that is 2 or 3 minutes long. One of the mistakes we have seen with existing large advertisers is that they think they are limited to 30 seconds (as they are used to advertising on TV). With these adverts the viewer is being forced to watch your initial 6 seconds before they can go on to watch the video they searched for. Remember here as well, that you've dropped an advert into someone's feed and they didn't ask for it, therefore they are likely to skip (but you are at the front of the view and they are forced to watch so this is great for brand awareness). Lots of brands are currently running a 15—20 second advert into these slots.

**Bumper adverts:** Again, these are initially non-skippable and up to 6 seconds, which a viewer will have to watch before being able to skip and then move on to see the main video, the same rules apply as above.

**Sponsored Cards:** These provide content relevant to the video, for example, products featured in the main video.

*Note:* When advertising on YouTube you may see the words *TrueView*. This is Google and YouTube's term and means that you only pay for a view once someone has watched more than 29 seconds of your ad. You have therefore received a 'true view' that had value—you've had a good chance to educate your potential customer. This sets Google/YouTube apart from Facebook and others (where you pay for impressions or even scroll past views, sometimes below the fold). Other platforms are pushing a TrueView offering, but debate continues around whether Facebook or others will follow.

If you are going to run non-skippable ads as either, pre or mid-roll you'll need to ensure 3 things: you have a very strong creative, your audiences have been nailed and that you hold the viewer's attention for the full 15 seconds. You'll be paying on a CPM (cost per thousand impressions) basis and bidding against other advertisers for viewable impressions.

When you're running TrueView ads it's a great opportunity to also run discovery and display campaigns (both of which are also TrueView, in that they are only paid for by you once someone clicks the ad, rather than paying for impressions). The whole *'impression based'* model is being brought into question and many advertisers are moving significant portions of their budgets over to TrueView in order to guarantee themselves and their brand value.

Most importantly though, make sure you hook people into your creative early. Get the brand in as quickly as possible, but remember, it will be the quality of your creativity, coupled with the audience design, that will determine the results coming out the back end of the campaigns.

Start with a wider audience than you may have thought you'd prefer initially, work hard on the data and don't rely too much on the automated tools that are there to encourage your wallet to open wide. All of the above will be trumped by creating an emotional connection with the audience. Google is measuring your retention and engagement—focus there and you'll win.

Never forget though, once you have people hooked, don't forget to tell them what to do next. Tell them the point of the campaign, steer them in the right direction, show clearly (without expectation) what you want someone to do next. Don't presume people know what you expect them to do, make it super clear, make sure your landing pages are fully optimised (following split testing different creatives), show them step by step where you want them to take action.

Storytelling is a great opportunity to take people along a funnel, and something not many people in advertising are talking about when discussing the tactics on YouTube. The barriers to entry being, in the first place, that you need a video, but when you want to fully educate potential customers you need several videos. Within the Google/YouTube platform you have the tools to show people a different video based on their action taken during video 1.

This is super powerful. Imagine showing video 1, those that skip can be shown video 1 again and if they skip again, they are now shown another video containing more information about the product in a different way. As people absorb information in different ways, the second piece of creative could, for instance, be substantially different visually or have more impactful audio> Let's call that video 2.

Those that then skip video 2 are removed completely from the ongoing campaign. Those that do watch past 30 seconds of video 1 can be segregated and shown another video, we'll call this video 3, and so on. So, you can actively take potential customers on a complete journey.

The issue is, you need to first scope out the journey and build the creative, meaning you may need to have 5 or more videos ready. There is, in theory, no limit to the number of videos you could show people. So, say for instance you've started with a really broad audience, you can narrow it down while warming up people along the journey. The people that make it three or four steps along the funnel are then ready to take action (they are there to be hit hard with offers, CTAs (call-to-actions), further creative etc. as we know they have bought into the product and brand). We also know we are not wasting advertising budgets when hitting these potential customers. Building these funnels and customer journeys is fascinating, and I firmly believe there will be people with '*specialist funnel design*' within their job descriptions, along with '*audience designer*'; bringing psychology into these disciplines will also be extremely important.

## How to structure your approach to YouTube Ads

As a basic framework you can look to use the following:

*The process below could take a lot longer than quoted. As an example, if you're a bigger brand some of these steps could take several weeks on their own. Conversely you may have some of these things in place already, so the below is just a guide.*

**Week 1:** Take time to plan your strategy and KPIs

**Week 2:** Define audiences, produce customer profile, script videos

**Week 3:** Produce and edit videos plus supporting materials

**Week 4:** Setup the funnel, put in place all tracking and test conversions

**Week 5:** Launch first set of adverts

**Week 6 to Week 8:** Test, learn, reiterate, gain insights—TAKE NOTES

**Week 8 to Week 10:** Further testing, learning

Remember to cast a reasonably wide net in the first instance and avoid the temptation to appeal to niche markets in the beginning, as they will return a lower customer rate.

The first objective with your campaigns should be to get them to break even and return £1 for every £1 spent. This is the first signal that you've got a campaign and ad sets that will perform well in the long term with profitability, we are of course looking for the best possible return. Playing the game and testing extensively is what will ensure that.

Within these campaigns that are generating a return there will be winning ads, winning audiences and certain demographics that are beginning to show themselves as better than the others inside the campaign. Now, the important thing is that you don't believe all this data to be '*proof*', yes, I've banged on about the data all along and sticking to the rules and what I've just typed may seem odd.

The amount of data you have is the all-important thing here. If you've only tested with a limited budget then you will most likely find that many of your placements, audiences, topics or keywords simply haven't had many (if any) impressions, meaning that you've learned nothing from these variations that sit within the campaign.

Step one here is then to split out the winning elements and duplicate out your campaign without the winning pieces of the puzzle—this gives you two campaigns to test against each other, effectively splitting out the audiences and placements that are yet to be tested.

Doing this you will need to double your budget and observe the campaigns over the next 7 to 10 days. Patience is key as it takes Google a while to learn and choose placements for you (based on your budgets), and then we are looking for conversions to show. Again, the budget and volume of impressions makes an enormous difference in how quickly you are able to gain enough data in order to make sure that you're judging like with like. My best advice here is to make extremely detailed notes and set out your planned objectives so that you can measure your own success.

One thing that I've observed often during this testing phase is a distinct pattern. You'll see days where campaigns perform amazingly well, followed by troughs; where you think to yourself *'what on earth went wrong, yesterday we had tons of conversions and I thought I had cracked it, now it looks like the campaign is a poor cousin of the one I had?'.* It's definitely a pattern that we see regularly in these testing phases and is perhaps, a reason why many agencies give up with YouTube Ads, as they lose faith before the campaign has had a chance to mature.

It is not unusual to see ups and downs with dramatic peaks and troughs over the first few weeks of campaigns on YouTube. What you are looking for is a trend upward though and to increase your conversion percentages when compared to impressions. Once you can get to 100+ conversions inside a campaign then the algorithm will have a much more consistent delivery. Again, all of this is subject to budget, competition and how aggressive you are with your bidding strategy.

A word of warning though, there is a setting in Google Ads which says *'Maximise conversions'*. You'd think that this is there to aid advertisers to get as many conversions as possible right? Wrong, it is a setting that if switched on simply tells Google to *'Spend all my budget please'*, yes choosing that setting will force Google to spend your budget. Useful in some circumstances, as sometimes we see campaigns not gaining any traction whatsoever or delivering any impressions.

My advice if you ever want to use the '*Maximise Conversions*' setting, split your campaigns down into many smaller budgets and always do this with a strategy that means you can learn quickly. But be prepared to accept losses during the use of this setting. We have seen some very good results with max conversions, normally though when setting the campaign budget at £10 or £15 per day and having lots of smaller campaigns with very focused audiences.

One of the big takeaways from this book, hopefully, will be that you are able to combine audiences and topics OR audiences and keywords, once you realise the power of the targeting opportunities and how to target that moment of intent. You'll see it's so much more powerful than the basic automated or '*smart*' campaign settings that Google will serve up to the inexperienced advertiser.

I can't teach you the exact science as there isn't a set of rules to follow. If there was everyone would be doing it, right? The general principles are that you have to trust the data and then compare that against your hypothesis.

It's a fascinating world of opportunity, so many different strategies exist that you'll no doubt learn things that I will never see. Each ad professional working at that level will have discovered insights from their data and methods that work for them and them alone. The rules are there to be bent, moulded and used to your advantage, it's an ever changing game. I've likened Google Ads to a complicated game of poker, and it is a game, we are all learning, playing, testing and moving. Just don't go 'all-in' unless you've got all that data and testing to back your decisions without a flicker of doubt (especially if it's not your media spend you are playing the game with).

How much of a budget do you need to get involved with testing then?

It's always a question that comes up, currently you'd need a budget of around £30—£50 a day to get a campaign to produce results, that said we have clients that spend significantly less. If you're really serious about it, then to run three or four campaigns you'll need £3-4K a month and to commit to running campaigns for at least 3 months (that means you are then into £10K+). It has to be thought of as an investment though and you should be able to build a consistent model that delivers positive and profitable ROI over that testing/learning phase, then, and only then, you get to scale.

I was asked recently by a business owner (who has a current turnover in the UK of £5M+ a year with a very well-known brand in his sector), what I thought I could scale his business to over the following 12 months. The answer I gave was simple, with the right investment I said we could easily treble his turnover. It wasn't an answer I gave without having researched his brand, the competition, the market and how much others were spending on ads.

My team had already spent a fair bit of time across social and found out how much the sector as a whole was worth. We also knew his current spend was minimal and he was No.3 in terms of brand awareness. We were confident his was actually the best product, it was just the marketing that was lacking, as the business owners had come from a non-digital background. They simply didn't have enough confidence or experience with digital to scale. Building that confidence was key, so starting small was the way forward. Luckily the business owner was a qualified accountant, so I knew that when the numbers supported my predicted outcome, then trust would be built, and the required investment would follow.

It's very exciting to see business growth like this, as proving a model is why I find it so rewarding, also finding the anomalies in campaigns and audiences is particularly important and satisfying. I am hoping those who may be reading this, who are like me, those that love the numbers and data and find joy in proving their hypothesis right. Those creative types that are reading this and thinking that you cannot think of anything worse, think that diving into the data is their special type of hell on earth, well, just remember you need those of us who live for the data, unless of course you fancy a go at it? Nope, I didn't think so. Thank your lucky stars there are some of us that are your extreme opposites.

Maybe that is why I get on with Andy so well—he produces some of the best creative work I've ever seen. He's even starting to enjoy the data, not just designing. Yes the creative is just as important, maybe the most important part, but measuring success and knowing what worked and why, should always be something that then leads into the next rounds of creative work; a collaborative approach is a must.

For far too long agencies, clients and departments have all worked separately from one another, sometimes siloed, but when you tie in all the data, creative, UX, conversion diagnostics, remarketing, funnel, sales, branding and everything else together, that is when the magic happens. I genuinely hope that going into 2022 and beyond we have a more transparent approach to marketing across all disciplines. The world has changed massively and so will the ways clients and agencies work together, hopefully more as a partnership than a retained relationship. We shall see.

Pinning down how this all works is difficult, the challenges can therefore be coming from all directions. Budgets, departments, managers, clients, temptations, patience—so much to deal with and take into account. This is where we need to bring in mindset and belief.

Mindset is going to matter, back this up with WRITING IT ALL DOWN. Obviously, you can make excuses to management, clients or even yourself, but we don't want any of that to be going on. Now we are back to reliance on the data and the KPIs you set at the outset, again removing the doubt and guesswork, removing the temptation to take rash decisions or seek the 'magic silver bullet' which is the cure all. We don't want to have a gamblers attitude. It's easy to get addicted to gambling purely because that big payday is right around the corner and just takes one great bit of luck (but in the mind it's never luck, right?).

The mindset of the successful advertiser includes at its heart, consistency. Consistently generating results, consistent action brings results, sticking to the plan and process brings results. Taking the guesswork out of the process is the important thought to have.

As you go on and derive more and more data from your campaigns through testing, that data gained will breed intelligence, brainpower in ad campaigns leads to better decisions and a strong mindset. Once you are winning and getting results, you'll consistently grow in confidence. Don't break the process and bring in doubt or guesswork by not following the data. I'm sure there are tons of people out there who can teach a strong mindset. Start with a system and be consistent, you'll then gain trust, but remember patience is the key to success.

## Once you are a winner

Having defined your parameters for success at the start, it's reasonably easy to be confident in scaling up your spend once you've hit your initial goals. Typically, we want to add 10-15% budget increases to winning ad-sets once they are performing at or above expectations.

The reason for adding slowly to the budget is because adding any more than this amount seems to disrupt the algorithm and asks it to learn too much too quickly. I like to think of it as a recipe for a cake, adding too much of one ingredient risks spoiling the mix, add gradually and you can keep control of the consistency. If you're in the mix with Google Ads, and particularly, with YouTube, you'll see that Google has a great feature where they will help you scale. It clearly shows how they feel a campaign can grow based on additional spend (note that they also show some nice little graphs next to their encouraging words), but remember it's a sales pitch. Google is in the business of getting you to spend as much as possible, as quickly as possible. Below you can see one of the illustrations Google shows at the point of offering to scale your campaign for you.

You will see that Google often lists campaigns as 'Limited by budget', then goes on to show something like this:

**Weekly estimates for your new daily budget:**

| Change daily budget | Weekly conv. | Weekly clicks | Cost / conv. | Weekly cost |
|---|---|---|---|---|
| US$2,000.00 | +18.4 | +2.25K | +US$16.33 | +US$2.61K |
| US$1,400.00 Recommended | +18.4 | +2.25K | +US$16.33 | +US$2.61K |
| US$800.00 | +8.7 | +1.14K | +US$7.87 | +US$1.2K |
| US$600.00 (current) | +0 | +0 | +US$0.00 | +US$0.00 |
| US$ | | | | |

Here we can see that the current daily budget for this particular campaign for one of our clients is $600. Google is kindly recommending a $1,400 daily budget which it says will result in an additional weekly spend of $2,610 or thereabouts. Stop a second though, if Google is recommending you spend an extra $800 a day, then multiply that by 7 days and that comes to $5,600, not $2,610! So, what is going on here? If we take a look at the suggested budget of $2,000 a day, we can see that there aren't any additional placements available (yet) as that also has a total additional spend of $2,610 for the week. Don't be fooled though, Google will 'save up' any unspent budget and keep it in the bank ready to spend should the opportunity arise. The issue is that should you run at $1,400 a day, Google isn't spending all the budget (even though you are encouraging Google to spend more). So at the end of the week there is budget saved up, perhaps as much as $3-4,000. I know I'm sounding like I'm going against logic here and, obviously, there could be a nagging doubt in the back of your mind saying "*Google must be right?*"—but NO, Google is simply showing you here the lazy man's way of going about things and as I have said in this book several times we don't want to be using all the off-the-shelf suggestions that Google provides.

We can, of course, garner some good insight from this suggestion that Google is making; we can see that there is room for growth and the ability to scale. My personal favoured option here would be to slowly increase the budget of the winning campaign by 10-15%, so if we are starting at $600 a day that means we can move to $660 or $690 (clearly nowhere near the suggested $1400), but we can increase this every 3-4 days based on continued success, and again in the similar increments so not to spoil the recipe. Then comes the question—"*What if you want to scale more quickly?*". That's where we need to have multiple campaigns, being careful to allow them to compete with each other. If you want to keep the same audiences and adverts you can simply duplicate your existing winning campaign, but so that it doesn't compete with it, you can do things such as, run the new one at a different time of day, choose a different set of placements, split winning audiences and so on. The goal being to build as many winning campaigns as possible, meaning you haven't got all your eggs in one basket.

There are arguments to say that you'd rather have 10 smaller campaigns than a couple of larger ones, this is however dependent on your budget. I've seen examples of clients where we have split a daily spend of £500 down into 25 campaigns (i.e. £20 per campaign per day) and observed that they massively out-perform the ones from previous months, where they were spending £150 a day on three campaigns.

This is obviously completely subjective, and every client is different. There are different numbers of available impressions, amount of competition, quality of creative, landing page experience... on top of another additional 50+ factors! So, I can't hope to give you a list of do's and don'ts here while you want to scale. It's not painting by numbers and that is what we rely on, in terms of being able to beat not just the algorithm, but the other agencies trying to outsmart it as well. A lot of this is gut, a good chunk is experience, testing comes into the mix and is the most important of the tools you have at your disposal.

The rules, the rules... testing, testing, testing and more testing. Backing yourself to get it right and being patient, being brave but not reckless. Make sure you are always learning and scaling within those parameters that I've talked about above, if you've got a high margin product and good conversion rates you may of course just want to press the rocket ship spend button that Google provides. Be prepared you'll grow quickly—just not at the same ROI as you would if you followed my rules.

Remember that testing equals intelligence and data. Great preparation and recording of your assumptions prior to beginning and then revisiting them will mean your campaigns will progress. Don't be afraid of making a few losses as the data gained is worth every penny. Also don't be disappointed when you do make a few mistakes, or campaigns don't meet your expectations; you can't win every time. You really do need to make a commitment for at least 3 months of hard work as it's not instant. Once campaigns are mature and predictable though, it is one of the most rewarding and stable advertising strategies that any business can deploy.

## Routine makes a massive difference

When you're managing an ad campaign, or several for that matter, it's super important that you get yourself into a routine.

It might be that you are only running three or four campaigns (we recommend you split test at least 3 different creatives and ideally 6, varying the calls to action, descriptions and ads), so you may only need to check how things are progressing every two or three days. With any number of creatives or ad sets that you are running, it's important not to become obsessed and check too regularly, as that will lead to mistakes and the temptation to make adjustments.

If you are going to be checking each of your campaigns every day, then try and do it at the same time each day, diarise all your findings and then build up to adjustments (don't be making adjustments on a daily basis, especially with campaigns that are still learning). Get into a routine that you know works. As I've just explained, we need to build up to making adjustments so that we don't sabotage the good work that has gone before. When you are making changes, don't make more than 2 or 3 every 3 days if you can help it. If you

are wanting to track properly then I'd suggest making notes of the following every time you visit your account:
- Campaign Name
- Ad-Set
- Advert (creative and type)
- Cost per view (CPV)
- Cost per 1000 impressions (CPM)
- Cost per conversion (CPA)
- Bid previous day
- Current bid
- Clicks through to site
- Winning audience notes

I also tend to keep an eye on some of the following dependant on the client or goals we are trying to achieve:
- Percentage view rate
- Video played to 50% percentage
- Video played to 100% percentage
- Optimisation score
- Estimated increase to scale
- Number of live placements
- Number of views in the last 7 days

There are tons more metrics you can keep an eye on obviously. You can, though, become 'stats blind' with too much information. So a word of warning, keep it simple to begin with and work towards your goals. What we primarily want to achieve are spot movements that come as a result of a previous round of adjustments and learning why that happened. When you do a bi-weekly or monthly review, then I'd suggest digging deeper, but this is something you cannot do on a daily basis as you'd end up in the matrix! Best practice would be to set up automated reports to come out of your account which have the greater levels of detail—but unless you have a team of data analysts at your disposal, or several hours to play with every day, don't get obsessed with the detail.

Some of the general rules of thumb are:
- Look for ongoing improvements in reach, clicks, conversions over the first 2-3 weeks of a campaign.
- Are conversions scaling in line with other metrics (are your conversions keeping pace with the growth in the placements, impressions and clicks)? Once you see a separation here, leave the campaign for 2 days and if there is no positive improvement then pause, copy and relaunch.
- If the campaign is more than 4 weeks old and performing consistently, are any of the current week's figures dropping off compared to the previous week?
- Are there any particular times of day, demographics, audiences, keywords or topics that are performing well—if so can we split them out into their own campaigns as a single topic/keyword campaign (SKAG). Think of this like when running a traditional PPC search campaign and you separate out single keyword ad groups as SKAG campaigns. These new campaigns get dropped into your winning buckets and are your seedlings to grow into mighty oaks.
- How many iterations of a campaign have there been? By that I mean, if you are on a third/fourth round of a campaign that you have already managed to get to perform, can we refer back and see any points at which the performance increased significantly, and what caused that success?

Remember, you can always refer back to the section within your ads account for each particular campaign and see the audit log of all your adjustments. I find it useful to refer to the graphical representations of campaigns over time, especially when looking for patterns (Google runs on patterns). If you can spot a pattern it may be that there is no clear explanation and the only conclusion you can draw, is that Google is phasing your campaigns. I've also explained this to clients in the past by saying that Google is doing this purely to see if you are paying attention, and if you are not, it sees a signal to start delivering lesser performance (like relegating you from the Premier League and placing you a couple of leagues below)—again the algorithm is clearly stacked in Google's favour, well that is what the cynic in me would say. ▋

# ▶ Conversion Diagnostics | Simon

▶ Now, there's a fancy phrase, 'conversion diagnostics'. What we really mean in layman's terms is, *'working out what made money and what didn't'*. Finding out which campaigns worked and which under-performed. The important thing to remember is to set expectations at the outset, without a benchmark. Yes, you will see the winners, but will you know how successful or not you have been against targets?

Often clients I work with have very complex funnels, ones they've been developing and expanding over the years for particular products or services. The more complicated you make your funnel, the more fun you're going to have with tracking the conversions, and when I say 'fun', I mean you're likely making a rod for your own back if you don't set the tracking up properly from the very start. After all, the aim of the game is deciding what worked and what didn't. The best piece of advice I can give you in this respect is to make sure you TAKE NOTES and make as many notes as you can. If you ever try to unpick a customer journey or campaign without the notes, you'll quickly find that there are so many variables you have little or no chance of understanding what actually happened, that can lead to assumptions and we all know where that ends up.

Personally, I like to use Google Sheets alongside the actual campaign, taking notes as I build out the ads and collateral. Then as adjustments are made along the timeline, you can see how your ideas played out; this can be a fascinating and highly rewarding process. Building and then checking your concepts and ideas against the social content, your budget calculations and KPIs makes the job so much easier. Yes it takes extra work, but the learning process is hastened and as long as these notes are kept correctly, it's easier at any point in the future to go back and see what adjustments you made to campaigns and how they affected the data in the following days.

There are loads of fancy systems out there for tracking your conversions and looking into what worked and what didn't. I've seen many of the top professionals using all sorts of systems. The bottom line is that many of them just use Google Sheets or good old Excel. There's pretty much nothing you can't make in Excel in terms of modelling campaigns and timelines, but maybe that makes me a dinosaur! I suppose it actually depends on the amount of data you want to see in a heads-up view, also how much of that data do you want other stakeholders to see?

Are you reporting what the customer or other members of your team want to see and what they care about? Keeping it simple is always best, then diving down into the weeds if the needs arise.

For me, the most important data is going to be conversion value vs media spend in order to give a customer acquisition, then all you need to know is if the conversions were of sufficient quality. That said, I've worked on many campaigns where brand awareness and impressions are seen as more important to some clients.

The key is to make sure that however your campaigns are set up, you can track them end-to-end and then, does that give you the ability to improve them moving forward?

Other clients like to focus on the number of eyeballs on their content, watched hours of their videos, event registrations or perhaps, click-through rates to their website landing pages. Maybe you or your client just want to get in front of your competitors' customers. What you need to make sure you've done is match your success calculations against your goals that were set prior to the inception of the campaign, did you hit the KPIs and goals?

Then you can compare and learn whether your assumptions about the audience and the course of action in your adverts resulted in your expected conversion rates. That's true conversion diagnostics.

## Letting the Algorithm Learn

Likes and dislikes don't matter. Concentrate on engagement and keeping people on your videos. If people are fast forwarding you'll get penalised by the algorithm, but more interestingly if people are rewinding and rewatching parts of your video again, then you get rewarded. Imagine a scenario where someone finds your video so good they watch it twice—200% engagement! If you can get a video to go viral or have really funny or surprising elements then that's going to make a big difference. Teaching people also works, 'how-to' is the most searched term with intent on YouTube. Imagine a scenario where you say in a video, '*I'm going to go through this quickly and teach you a few really good things, make some notes*', then what is going to happen is people are going to pause, rewind, rewatch and this all contributes to great retention rates and getting people to stay, giving YouTube a great signal in terms of retention.

Google laps up the signals, it's only a bot and these are the only things that it can learn from.

Lots of people will 'skim' through content occasionally, another great little trick is to have visual summary sections such as 'menu cards', then when viewers spot these cue cards they pause. Then they look for the point that they are interested in and rewind to that point, watch again; these are signals to YouTube that watchers are loving the content. See if you can think of innovative ways to get people to watch your video more than once, that's real gold dust if you can achieve more than 100% watch rate.

If your video is seen as more of an authority and an engaging piece it will be promoted internally by YouTube. Getting into the 'Suggested videos' section is a big success and this is where 90+% of the traffic for organic videos and viral videos will come from. Your content may then be featured on Google Search if it's judged valuable, interesting and engaging—you just won the X-Factor, now you are getting organic traffic from a video that might have begun life as an advert.

Many of the videos that feature in the main search are there for years pulling in traffic and enquiries for their publishers. So, don't think of YouTube advertising as just a means to drive enquiries or sales from paid media, it can dominate in the search listings and drive more traffic your way too.

Another great tactic is to get your links built into your videos, linking through to other videos on your channel while your video is playing will further engage the viewers and give more great signals to YouTube. You can do this through the use of cards which are an option when publishing your YouTube videos. The best bet is to try and drive someone onto another video within your channel that is also relevant.

If you're running ads and also trying to build an organic channel, there could be an argument to say you should split out your ads channel from your organic videos. However, if your adverts are short (1 to 3 minutes) then retention should be good once people start watching them.

For example, you wouldn't want to pay to promote a really long video (unless it was to a very specific audience or search term) as you may well get lots of skips at the start within the first minute, and therefore your retention rate for the overall video would be small and could perhaps affect your channel in the long run. This is an interesting and ongoing debate among YouTube ads and channel growth experts. There's no real clear answer currently. My opinion is that you'd test the retention rates, as long as your targeting is accurate, and run ads that are interesting and relevant which will maintain a good retention rate and of course drive clicks and sales. There is a balance between ads and organic, and there are also long and short-term considerations for your channel. Once you commit to building a big organic channel you'll need to decide if you are planning on adding to it consistently. I see a change coming to YouTube, it will become a more collaborative place with influencers and brands building content together, promoting each other, knowing their audiences, sharing, and retaining them, YouTube rewarding both as a result.

Of course, we all want our campaign and channel to work together and get to the place where we know that your campaigns will convert consistently all day long and can be scaled further and further and further until you hit a plateau. This takes time, but in reality, should take 3-6 months. It is a case that you may well need to spend tens of thousands of pounds to get your account to a point where Google will allow it to scale properly i.e. YouTube and Google want to see that your business is serious and you are prepared to commit to long-term advertising. The flip side of this is, if Google allowed just anybody to come into the market with a new product and advertise and come above you, that wouldn't really be fair, as you've been a customer for a long time, would it?

Google's a business and they are going to look after their long-term committed customers, to get into that group you need to commit and not treat YouTube ads as a magic bullet or short-term win.

On top of all of this sits the need to stay ahead of all the tools and latest practice guidelines, I'd highly suggest you go and take the Google Ads exams. Go to the Skillshop, follow through with as much of the training as you can, take some of the YouTube Ads courses as they are particularly relevant.

There's nothing quite like producing your own ads and getting them running, then testing them, tweaking them, learning, adjusting, reiterating, relaunching, trying new budgets, adjusting your creative, looking at the analytics, insight and data that comes out of the backend—all of that is absolutely fascinating—well it is to me! If you don't fancy doing all that then get a professional on board, just make sure it's not one of the 'Illegitimate Experts' out there, you know, those people that talk a very good game but have no real 'game' to back it up, selling their little courses or special systems.

They are mainly the ones selling the courses and claiming to be the 'world's best' and have made millions for their clients. Modern day carnie operators, selling 'unicorn potions' which achieve the 'hack of the century' or beat any other ad in the history of advertising, or OTTERS as I call them, 'Over The Top Exaggerated Returns Sellers', watch out they are slippery little buggers!

## View-Through and Analytics

One of the important metrics that you're going to need to look at when analysing your YouTube ads, as well as your organic videos, will be the length of time that people spend watching the video itself.

A shorter watch rate (better known as a retention rate) will possibly have a detrimental implication and damage your channel organically. This can be mitigated when running adverts on YouTube by running your advert as an unlisted video. This is a good tactic because when a video is left as unlisted, it will not impact your overall channel analytics.

We always need to remember that THE single most important thing Google is bothered about is engagement. If someone bounces off your video you will be giving poor signals and your costs increase. If this happens consistently, then you will pay more for your ads, struggle to get traction and your competition will have a significant advantage if their content is better received.

If a video is made public and used as an advert we need to focus on making sure that the audience is designed properly, again this is done to increase the engagement and give good signals to Google. It's a very attractive tactic for advertisers to run videos which are adverts on their channel, the channel owner then has videos in their playlists with very high view numbers (assuming there is a decent budget being assigned to promotion). This could mean videos popping up on the homepage of your channel showing tens, if not hundreds of thousands, of views as the public cannot tell the difference between a paid for and organic view—it just appears that you have an incredibly well watched channel. If you have paid to advertise a video as a brand, the important balance you need to strike and take into consideration is the trade-off between the length of the video and the engagement of that video—we want our viewers, be they consumers served the content via an advert or those finding the content organically, to stay on the video as long as possible. Good times for Google, lower cost to advertise for you, now and in the long term.

Clearly the goal of all of us as channel owners is to get as many people to watch as much of our content as possible, we want them to stay and interact with other videos on our channel which in turn, will help us gain a healthy engagement rate; this is much like old school SEO but for video. It then stands to reason that if your targeting is poor, or your video quality is low, or your audience definition isn't as good as it could be, your watch rates will go down.

Then, for example, you will see a smaller and smaller percentage of your video being watched. This is easy to check with the analytics available in the back of Google Ads by clicking the views selector in campaign reporting, or within your YouTube studio, where you can also see how your videos are performing organically. Within your Google Ads suite, you can set up your reporting in order to see how many people watched 25%, 50%, 75% and 100% of your video.

The question that always comes up following this is, "*What's a good watch percentage?*". Ultimately, the answer depends on how long the video is. Clearly, it's easier to get someone to watch all of a 1-minute video than it is the entirety of a 10-minute video, that's why watch time is also important as a metric, pay attention to that as the secondary metric. Therefore, it follows that the longer your video, the harder it will be to get people to watch it all, but that being said it is far more valuable to get people to watch 7 minutes of a 10-minute video than 55 seconds of a one-minute video (unless of course those exact figures were replicated across every single viewer of your video, which is of course not going to play out in the real world).

So, what is a good watch through percentage?

When running adverts that are in the region of 3 to 5 minutes in length, I'm looking to get more than a quarter of the viewers past half way, that's giving me the signal that the audience is decently profiled. I've checked a client campaign this morning and they are getting 34% of viewers to the end of a 5 minute ad/video. That is showing me we are beginning to really dial in the audience for that client—again this is all subjective as it varies wildly with different offers, products, audiences and bids.

Once you can see your retention rate and overall watch time, it's important to get the balance of the creative and the length of video right. Always keeping front of mind that people need to stay engaged and therefore be able to maintain a consistent watch rate. If you see too many of your viewers diving off the video or skipping straight away, either your audience isn't correct, your creative isn't engaging, or your video simply doesn't have the hooks and calls to action in the right places. There's also an argument to say that if people are jumping off your video they may well be clicking through to your website before having watched through to the end of the video, which would obviously be a good sign providing they are then taking action upon landing. YouTube gets paid if you receive a click to your website even if that happens within the first 29 seconds (I'd be very rich if I got £10 for every time a client said to me 'let's just make the advert 29 seconds long then').

Landing page experience is then crucial, you need to be concerned about the following:
- ▶ Does the traffic that is clicking through from your adverts take action?
- ▶ Do they stay on the page or navigate around to other parts of your site?
- ▶ What elements of the page are they interacting with?
- ▶ How long on average are they staying on the page?
- ▶ Do they enquire?
- ▶ Do they make a purchase?

We absolutely don't want people landing, then bouncing off the page and not getting what they expected to find.

Having watched your video there are certain expectations generated for your viewer, therefore it's a good idea to make sure that the landing page experience ties up nicely with what you were offering in the video. This may seem obvious, but I've seen many, many, sites place an ad and get people to click through and then experience very high bounce rates purely because the experience in the video is nothing like the experience when they land on the landing page.

Simply making sure fonts, colours, logos etc. are the same are the basics. But the headlines, offers and calls to action all need to be taken into account, often the only way to get it right is to test different pages.

Another good tip is to look at other advertisers in your same market who are spending significant amounts of money on adverts over a period of time, presumably they have dialled in their landing pages and offers. Look for a theme, are they all doing it the same way? Is there a particular way of setting up the pages for success?

We absolutely want people to convert once they land on the destination page. The difference between a great landing page and one that doesn't convert anywhere near as well as it could be is massive, you either have a 'campaign killer' or a 'heroic converter'.

I've seen tons of great traffic to pages only failing to convert because the calls to action or form on the page are in the wrong place. Equally I've had clients tell me their landing page converts at 30% and they close nearly every enquiry into new business. Those are illusions and often come from people at the top of an organisation that clearly have no real perception of the data.

Furthermore, you want to give Google good signals, including time on site and consistent conversion data. Always remembering we want 50 or so conversions per campaign per month to teach the AI, that is what allows you to eventually swap to target cost per acquisition bidding. The very first step in these campaigns is to make sure you have tags built-in to track the conversions. This is absolutely crucial as it means that Google gets as many good conversion signals as possible from your ads. Data to Google is everything, teach your campaigns and you will be rewarded, but if you are lazy and don't build in the tracking it will mean that your competitors' adverts are preferred or perhaps you will pay double or treble what you should or could be paying in the long-term.

Google Tag Manager is the go-to choice for building those signals, as always when you have the option to use a Google tool with a Google product such as YouTube. Bottom line is, and I can't emphasise it enough, you must teach Google what is a success (starting with any success, not necessarily a sale to begin with, as we can teach Google about all sorts of valuable events), what is a conversion, what worked for you, did Google do a good job, if so, tell it.

Make sure you always teach Google's AI how you expect your advert to perform. All of that prized conversion data and the values get fed back into Google Ads Manager and your campaigns conversion events, tying in all the events you set up. Make sure that value ties up with the actual amount that your business receives from the particular conversion you set, meaning that you can easily be able to compare revenue driven from ads, to the cost of the corresponding media spend, giving you an accurate ROI. One last thing to bear in mind, you'll want to consider the lifetime value of the customer on top of this simple conversion metric—it's not always just about CPA vs sale, especially when trying to grow your customer base.

One of the easiest ways to test conversions and watch rates, and I'd suggest you do this in all of your ad campaigns if you're running ads on YouTube through Google Ads, would be to run at least three different videos as adverts in the one campaign. This enables you to be able to see differences (subtle differences) between different video ads, ideally you would run 6 different ads in the same campaign with different calls to action, different call-out text, different URLs and different ad extensions. You'll be able to gain enough insight over a period into which ads work and why. It may be that it's as simple as, the words that are spoken in the first few seconds make all the difference, it might be that a shorter, punchier ad is the way to go. Once you can gain this sort of knowledge as to how your audience is responding to your adverts and creative, you're able to continually improve, reiterate, and run more ads.

It's important to bear in mind that when Google runs an ad that it's not as simple as letting an advert run infinitum. Ads always suffer from 'advert fatigue', maybe this is because your audience has been exhausted, or your creative is becoming less engaging, maybe there is something in the backend of Google that says *"hey, these guys have just left their ad running for 4 weeks and not made any changes, let's take some of their budget and deliver less impressions"*.

Google wouldn't do that would they, surely not?

Simply by spinning up a new ad or changing the copy of an existing ad that is suffering from fatigue then relaunching, Google will then often reinvigorate the same set of ads, giving you new traffic, new conversions, new customers, more impressions and lower costs. The Google Ads game is not just as simple as a set and forget—that's the route to wasting a whole shed load of budget over the long term.

Campaigns require ongoing work, note making, testing, planning and strategy. If they didn't, then people like myself and my business would clearly not exist.

Scaling consistently is something that Facebook struggles with. I don't know if that is to do with audience sizes or something more sinister, I've seen campaigns that are amazingly successful on Facebook fall off a cliff once people try to scale them, more often than not this is because people try to go too quickly and believe that they've got to a point where they can just scale from 100 to 300 to 700 to $1,000 a day, when in fact, Facebook would have responded more favourably had you just added, for example, 10% of the budget every other day.

For those of you wanting to scale, adding little and often is far better than lumping on more than 15-20% additional budget, that goes for Facebook and Google.

Think of it like this, if you double your budget, how likely is it that the AI will double the impressions with the same quality of traffic you currently have in a winning campaign? Best case scenario is that good quality impressions are added after a few days, in the meantime you are spending to let your campaigns learn and pay for the privilege.

Better to scale by adding slowly, watching the results and then adding again. Once you have added some budget to a campaign and not raised it too quickly you should let your ad settle back into a rhythm for about 3 days, learn, and then scale again.

When you start to see ads dropping off in performance, clicks, engagement and view rates, you're able to then spin-up new ads with slight tweaks and improvements and let Google learn again. You are not learning from ground zero though, Google helps by bringing in the knowledge from your previous campaign and your new ones will out-perform the previous batch and deliver more results.

One of the biggest considerations with this type of ad placement is patience. You do need a budget to be able to test and learn, either that or you need to be extremely lucky and get your first set of ads absolutely perfect, but there can always be improvements made by refining your audiences, topics and placement selections. Yes, it's one long drawn-out battle to win against Google, but it is extremely rewarding when you get it right.

One of the principal mistakes I see a lot of people make is tying up Google Analytics as their goal tracking solution, it doesn't respond anywhere near as well as Google Tag Manager and the data is harder to interpret. We could have a debate for hours about tracking solutions and first to last click attribution models.

For fear that nobody will read that apart from the true geeks let's skip to the chase and say this: *"There is no perfect tracking solution out there, no two tracking systems for conversions will ever show exactly the same data, the best solution is to compare all sources and allocate what you think is the single version of the truth"*—when you are deep in a campaign and running it day to day as a Google Ads professional, often it's gut feel and knowing your audiences inside out that really matters and makes the biggest difference.

My conversion tracking of choice and insight in terms of on-site data is Google Tag Manager, there's plenty of videos out there on the web of how-to setup Google Tag Manager properly, what to track and how, let it track everything from phone calls, to page visits, to purchases, form fills, how long someone watched a video on your site, pretty much everything you want, including your Facebook tags and everything in between.

## Pixels, tracking

Tracking, tracking, more tracking and yes, more tracking. It's hard to not overstate the importance of putting all the tracking in place BEFORE you go ahead and launch any campaigns, why? Because we must be able to teach the algorithms and let them learn what a good result looks like.

All of the online advertising tools, including Google, Facebook, LinkedIn etc. afford you the possibility of being able to fully track every action your potential client/customer takes when interacting with your ad campaigns. Some of the actions you may want to track are:
- Sales (by value)
- Registrations
- Downloads
- Enquiries
- Telephone Calls
- Other on-site actions

Another great reason for putting in place the tracking pixel or code is to enable remarketing, additionally this can then be cross platform (creating lookalike and expanded audiences).

Testing, learning, reiterating and then testing again. If you put in place a full suite of tracking, then the data and insight we can learn from enables better decision making. All too often the temptation is to leave a campaign to run, especially when it is delivering a level of success, but if you have the right data, then continual improvement should be achievable. You'll not attain this without a test-learn-reiterate-reasoning approach, based on the data and your detailed notes as to why you made the changes.

It's established practice to let the algorithms learn. They learn through the data, when a conversion is achieved then the systems behind Google, Facebook and other huge corporations see that as a result, and are, therefore, then able to find more people who match the profile of the person who just converted on your advert. However, it is not as simple as that, let me try and explain as this is where things get a whole lot more complicated, very quickly.

Let's say your goal is a sale, that one is easy, you optimise for the conversion event of the 'thank you' page—job done, right? Well, yes, eventually. The issue is, you cannot optimise from day one for that conversion, the AI has no data to base its decisions on. Google for example, wants roughly 100 conversions to base its decisions on, and as the number of conversions increases, so does the ability for the algorithm to match people to those that work best for your business.

So, how do we achieve that 100+ conversion figure? Take a step back and look at the audiences. No doubt if you have done a thorough job on defining the initial customer profile then you are on your way to success. But we need to look at what could be the initial conversion events we want to track (with the aim of ending up with a single conversion goal of *'sales'*). The first step is to look at getting our audience to take action and visit our site and spend time on site (where we are talking an e-commerce example), having been exposed to an advert or set of ads within a funnel. I've outlined some basic examples below:-

**Step 1:** Initial audience sees video advert one.
- ▶ (we observe how many people watch past 50% of this advert)

**Step 2—Some people click through to the site**
- ▶ (this can be an initial conversion event, although low level signal)

**Step 3:** A small percentage of this initial audience browses around the site, some convert to a sale, some may make contact in other ways (phone calls and form fills), all of which are other conversion events worth measuring in the initial stages of the campaign.

**Step 4:** Those that watched more than 50% of video advert one, are shown video advert 2.

**Step 5:** Question: Are the conversion percentages higher in the second advert trial?

**Step 6:** Test further audiences and creative.

**Step 7:** Learn and refine audiences based on those that are hitting initial conversions.

**Step 8:** Move those that are engaging with the first sets of adverts into a new audience
- (If the new audiences are large enough it will allow similar audiences and audience expansion to be brought into the campaigns)

**Step 9:** Remarket to those that have already engaged, maybe use an initial launch offer at this point to encourage them to convert (ask yourself if you do this, should these lower value converters be a different audience).

**Step 10:** Analyse results, take stock and plan next steps.

If your budgets are big enough, this initial activity may have achieved your goal of 100 sale conversions target in order to begin using the AI features properly. We do need to caveat the use of the algorithms though, remember the real goal they have is to keep you spending, so whatever anyone says, it is a continual game to play and not a *'set and forget'* tool once these 100 goals are achieved.

With that in mind, one other thing to mention is that ads and campaigns can suffer from fatigue, those cycles only become apparent once an account matures over a number of months, but as a rule I'd suggest not leaving an advert running more than 3 or 4 weeks without refreshing it, or before if you see a 3 day drop in performance.

The other thing we have to be aware of, is not being tempted into optimising for negative conversions (we don't want to set conversion goals that end up being valueless). As an example of this we could look at an audience of *'people who click through to the website but fail to purchase'*. There could, of course, be many reasons why someone doesn't buy once they land on the site (again we need enough data for the data to be statistically meaningful). We may not want Google/Facebook to send us more people who land and then don't buy.

What you can often find though (and learn), is that these visitors may well just need further warming up, more information and to be taken further down the funnel. Remember, these initial people have come from a cold audience, so it is also well worth noting at what stage these people are at in the funnel, they will still be valuable. Testing offers and remarketing to this audience is essential.

The testing phase of campaigns and warming up of audiences against conversions is one of the hardest parts of digital marketing. We do live in a culture where immediate gratification is expected and often clients go into campaigns thinking that they will deliver from day one. Hopefully you can see that by splitting out and letting the algorithms learn, you are learning more about the data yourself and therefore how enormously important testing is. It takes patience, budgets, data, learning, more testing and eventually you can get to a position where campaigns are scalable with a level of certainty.

Having a wider set of conversion goals at the top of the funnel makes it much easier in the long run to understand the behaviour of your engaged users. Be careful though to not let the algorithms think each of those conversions has an equal value.

Google has some nice tools in this respect. It allows you to assign a *'notional value'* to particular conversions. In the example I've given above, let's say we are selling a product that has a value of £100 (and within that £100 there is £35 profit), it's also a product that once someone becomes a customer they are likely to come back and buy more than once (from historical data), so we can assign a value of £70 profit, to the lifetime value of that client. The question then that rears its ugly head is *"how much of that £70 is the advertiser willing to give up in order to acquire that customer?"* Well the answer is obvious.... *'As little as possible'*. I wish I had a pound for every time I've heard that phrase come out of a client's mouth. The thing is, Google and Facebook etc. all want their fair share of the bounty; they absolutely see it that there is money to be made off you as the advertiser and space is at a premium. So, should we put a value of £100, £70, £35, £10 or pull any number out of the air when creating our campaign?

If we are going to follow the rules to the letter, then it may seem obvious to put a value of £100 on the sale conversion event wouldn't it? Do you want to tell Google that *"Great, when you give me a customer I make £100"*, well no, you are not making £100, you may be making a sale of £100, but your profit is £35, the lifetime value of that customer is £70 (profit). Now go back to the *"How much are we prepared to pay to acquire a customer"* question. From experience it may be reasonable to expect to give away 10-15% of your turnover on these types of advertising campaigns (I hear so much about ROAS—return on ad spend, but this takes no real consideration into account of PROFIT, or lifetime value of the customer). Equally all clients will not really let lifetime value come into a calculation unless they are a sophisticated business, so often we are then left with battling a spend versus turnover calculation. What should we enter then as a conversion value for Google? Confused?

To clearly answer that question, you need to understand the customer value and product properly, plus the goals of the campaign, only then can you decide where to pitch the campaign to Google. In the above example, we might want to tell Google that a conversion (sale of £100 with £35 profit) is worth £15 as a starting point. '*Woah*!" I hear people shouting, *"what are you doing Simon, that initial figure is 15% of the total sale"*. What we have to do is then see how well Google can deliver compared against our expectations. Obviously we would like the campaign to deliver these conversions at

£7 or even less, but this all comes back to and depends on how competitive your market is, how much profit is in the product, how much budget you have and how committed you are to push through to spend and learn.

If we are going to go with an initial 'guess' at a value of £15 and educate Google to optimise to that value, we might set other values (which are less valuable as previously discussed):
- Website visitor—£0.30
- Phone call—£3.00
- Brochure Download—£30

Those figures above are based on the following rules:-

We know that we have a traditional on-site conversion to sale of 2% for website visitors (one sale per 50 visitors to the site, 50 x £0.30 = £15, this is the overall conversion value divided by the number of people to achieve a conversion).

Phone calls (£3), this is because we know one in 5 phone calls turns into a customer in this particular client's account.

Brochure Download (£30), it may seem strange that this conversion is set to be more valuable than a sale, however we know that those clients that go onto the site and download a brochure tend to be the ones that buy multiple times and become long-term clients. Therefore, a higher value is assigned. This teaches Google that these people are even more valuable.

As you can probably see, this is where things can become extremely complicated. Google would ask you to just hook up the *'sale value'* and to be fair this is where 99% of advertisers will stick, they would set their conversion at £100, that being the cart total for a sale, as I say, that is a dangerous route and gives you very little wiggle room when it comes to *'negotiating'* a better deal with the advertisers, as you've laid all your cards out on the table from day one of the campaign.

Budget optimisation against conversion objectives is an ongoing strategy, don't expect the advertising platforms to deliver a ROAS of 8 or 10x just because you told them that was what you expected. Have fun with that. I expect you will be having some fun, your advantage is you have the knowledge of where your campaign needs to sit, you need to control the algorithm, not the other way around.

## Stopping Fraudulent Clicks

Google would tell us that each and every single click on an advert is examined by their system, and it has extremely sophisticated systems in order to identify any invalid or fraudulent clicks and remove them from your account. Well, I've got some news for you Google doesn't give a flying f*** about fraudulent clicks really. At the end of the day they get paid for every single click and yes, they may well be identifying fraud at a very basic level and removing an element of clicks that are deemed to be 'invalid', but as we stand, roughly 15 to 20% of all clicks that come through are most likely to be fraudulent, that's a big chunk of anyone's ads budget.

A good proportion of the clicks that are on Google Ads or Facebook and other social networks where you're paying media spend, are fraudulent. There's a whole enormous industry built up around (bots) clickbait and clicking competitors' ads. There are several well-known examples where fraudsters have created adsense websites in the thousands, then loaded them with ads, directed clicks and traffic to their sites and harvested advertiser's media budgets, some of the worst examples are in the millions of dollar's worth of fraud, and it continues at pace still to this day. It's the age-old example, if these guys are using the 'if I take 1 pence from every single person out there nobody notices' method, then very little can be done to stop them. They are skimming from the system and it's well known that Google isn't in the business of even really wanting to try and actively put a stop to this. They are after all making 50% or more on even the fraudulent activity. Come on Google, please put a stop to this, I'm sure you have the ability to clamp down on it should you wish to.

Around a year or so ago one of my clients was spending around £25,000 a month on their Google Ads account and we started to spot some very suspicious activity, suspecting a competitor was clicking on the client's advert regularly, we investigated further. We put a tool in place, only a basic one, called Clickcease.

The tool itself purely blocks multiple clicks from IP ranges, but it does allow you to see where your clicks are coming from. Having run the tool for a month it became obvious that certain IP addresses were making hundreds of clicks to the client's ads, consistently, all too regularly.

With this evidence in hand I approached Google and asked for a refund proportionate to the fraudulent clicks that they had received on their account, the initial response was;- "*We will put you through to the relevant team and they will investigate*", several weeks passed and then a response came back to say that they had investigated the account and they 'required further evidence' (which I was more than happy to provide having downloaded detailed reports from Clickcease), I thought I would be able back up my case.

As adults, we know that the real purpose of the request for further information, is to get rid of a good chunk of the complaints, as it's just another hurdle you have to negotiate, I pushed on. I then proceeded to send this further information over to Google and again waited.

A couple of weeks passed and then I received another email, apparently the matter now needed to be passed to an even higher authority (team), and I would have to wait for further investigation. In the meantime the customer is still continuing to pay his £25,000 a month to Google as his business was completely reliant on receiving ongoing traffic and leads. This really isn't fair in my mind, as the client was continuing, as far as we were concerned, to spend a proportion of his traffic coming from bots and his competitors clicking his ads, although the Clickcease tool did do somewhat of a job stopping to this (there are other such tools out there and my current favourite is PPC Protect).

My point is that we should not have to deal with this type of activity in the first place, and we shouldn't need to put all these tools in place to block IP addresses etc. Within the Google Ads platform itself you only have the option to block up to 500 of these suspect IP addresses, so God only knows how your average advertiser goes on to stop this fraudulent activity easily without paying for a tool. Therefore, most advertisers who fall in the sub £1,000 a month spend category, simply have to put up with knowing (or not knowing) that a percentage of their traffic is actually just bots and will never convert into business.

Back to my Advertiser who's account we are talking about, another few weeks passed and I then received an email asking for even more information. I replied saying that '*I had provided everything that I had*', and a week later I had a final decision. Google replied saying that they had fully investigated my claim and concluded that there was no fraudulent or bot activity within the clients account, no surprise there then!

So, are we all supposed to trust Google implicitly that they will investigate? I personally believe through this experience there was no actual investigation and a series of pre-programmed emails. We had to take Google's word and without any real human engagement, I had effectively been fobbed off.

I'm sure Google would deny that this is actually the case and the chances are maybe, just maybe, there are actual humans, actually looking at these types of complaints. But there must be a system which is in place to drive the majority of these complaints away in an automated fashion, then the robots can take the complaints about the robots and give you a robot response. It's laughable, but we are all beholden to the system. I'd just like a bit more transparency please.

I suppose when complaints get to a certain level of annoyance or potential liability for embarrassment, you then have to ask yourself is there a team at Google who do investigate serious complaints, where reclaims could constitute hundreds of thousands of pounds? Who has a different level of authority and skill to those that are tasked with dealing with a level of complaint at only a few thousand pounds a month? Take the average Google account manager as an example, many of them are purely salespeople, and in a position where, as I call it, their job title is actually 'Chief Wallet Opener', they must be on commission right? Let's be clear, in the main they are tasked with calling direct clients and agencies and offering solutions, not all of which, at the time I'm writing, will drive the results that the client is looking for. Many of these suggestions are 'off the shelf' or the 'latest and greatest new bidding strategies', all of which have one thing at their centre, they are designed to spend more money on ads, can you blame them? Maybe even they are on commission?

Of course they are there to get advertisers spending as much as possible, I've definitely said that before, but ask them some technical questions and the level of knowledge is not really there. Please draw your own conclusions, on a side note, if you're reading this book and you've had a similar experience, I'd love to hear from you so find me on LinkedIn, send me a message and let's chat. If you're working at Google and reading this then come to the agency side, I bet you'd learn more and have more fun.

There are some very good tools out there that can block fraudulent clicks, there are even some enterprise level solutions. My question is, should we really have to pay for these tools when Google could clearly put them there in the first place easily themselves? It's not all bad, and I am sure Google is getting better at stopping the bots, it's just that we live in a world where one solution is stopped and there is nearly always a workaround. From an advertisers perspective, you either take the rough with the smooth, or you build your campaigns to avoid all the bad placements where the bots live.

What can you do to put measures in place and stop these bot clicks yourselves?

The first thing to do is a look at where your clicks are coming from and if you're getting multiple numbers of clicks from particular sites or parts of the display network, this could be a decent signal that fraud is occurring.

Once you find a site or placement that you think could be producing a suspicious number of clicks on your ads, go check it out, the chances are once you look at the placement or site, it may well be a domain that has been registered in the last few weeks, or have an odd extension such as .xyz.

Follow it through and the page will normally have an inordinate number of adverts on it, couple this with extremely thin content, meaning that the website genuinely isn't there to provide any true value, and you will be looking at a fraudsters' money site. The best way to combat this is not to do it all manually, although it is a good idea to investigate any placements that seem to produce odd results. It's better to use exclusion lists; grow your own, as well as buy in or use public lists of bad placements.

Other signals to pay attention to are conversion rates. The bots are extremely clever nowadays in that they will even fill out your forms, scroll up and down your page, visit other parts of your site, making the traffic look extremely genuine, but if you look at sites that are producing conversions, it's highly unlikely that these particular placements or sites are producing very high conversion rates.

Why would bots bother to produce conversions? Well as we know Google teaches itself to go and get more conversions, so if they again make themselves look 'natural' then they don't get spotted as easily. These fraudsters know that if they can create conversions on your campaigns, Google begins to optimise and serve even more to their fraudulent sites and clicks, which becomes an ever-filling prophecy of doom. The more you spend the more you will fall into their trap, this is why we as advertisers need to continually query and question the placements within campaigns. This is particularly true in YouTube and the display network. If you are new to this, a good place to start is to exclude the entire app store and the display network.

Wait! I hear someone shouting, isn't this all a moot point, there are so many fraudulent sites out there that it is practically impossible to continually comb through your campaigns and eliminate the problem, it effectively could turn into somebody's full-time job. Hang on 1-minute, didn't I say that Google should be doing this job for us?

You can of course choose specific placements and trusted placements within the display network, that way at least you know you have limited where your ads show. So, in turn you will be less likely for the bots to target you, that however, does massively limit your reach, and if your potential customer is like a needle in a haystack, you've just taken 99% of the haystack away.

Chances are your customer is no longer there, but ho-hum neither are the bots and now your campaign doesn't work at all anyway, see the conundrum. The thing is this, with YouTube it's possible to get brilliant results if you haven't got much of a clue or you just use a 'spray and pray' approach. There are so few businesses using it right now that it's not hard to get results, it's just that there are certain things to look out for, and sitting back is never the best strategy. Continually improving your campaigns will always win in the long run and save you massive amounts of media spend.

We all want really accurate campaign data in order to base decisions on future marketing activity and unless you are going to work hard to exclude the fraudulent elements within campaigns, that data will be next to useless, so be careful and be vigilant, it is the lazy casual advertiser that falls victim most often to these bots and tactics. It is only akin to modern-day piracy, robbing from easy victims who leave themselves vulnerable. It's just that there are 1000s of Dick Turpin's out there, and the sheriff (Google) isn't going to protect you unless you take the appropriate measures.

## The Audience Manager

A whole new job role is coming and specifically it's your in-house '*audience manager*'. Yes, Google are following the model of making the tools easier to use for an average user, and they are enabling standard audiences at deeper and deeper levels all the time. But nothing is going to beat human intelligence.

Continual audience profiling and learning will always give you an advantage over the lazy advertisers that rely on the standard 'off the shelf' audiences that Google provides. Take this example, when Google spins up an audience for you the size and reach will be initially determined by your budget and location choice (providing there is a big enough pool to choose from), it will then select placements for your campaign.

Typically, there might be a few thousand placements for your campaign to begin serving ads into, but if your budget is limited (say under £100 a day to begin) you'll have no chance of serving your ads into the entire audience at any meaningful level to get decent data. The lazy advertiser sits back here and waits. What you'll observe as behaviour from Google at this point is most likely to be 30 or 40 placements dominating the ads spend, so unless they are immediately creating conversions at a good level, you are already burning budget (testing), so we don't want to leave a campaign alone to do its thing, do we? Well, the correct answer is that you really need to allow the campaign to run for a few days. Some can grab on day one, some may take several days to learn and grab, again this is determined by the audience and the competition, i.e. are you bidding for placements that are incredibly competitive. I've seen examples of campaigns with good budgets sitting there for more than 2 weeks on occasion and then grab.

At this point it is also important to remember that Google is 'saving up' your budget, meaning that if you set a campaign on £100 a day and nothing happened for 4 days, it has got £400 in the bank to spend, don't therefore be surprised if you then spend £200, £300 a day in subsequent days, so be warned, if you are running campaigns over a long period of time and they are not spending all the budget, then you run the risk of blowing it if you make sudden adjustments to CPV or CPM bids.

Back to the placements list, you've been running for a couple of weeks and have your ad groups served into a few hundred or thousand placements. You'll, as stated, most likely see some of the placements dominating. If they are not performing, you'll want to remove the ones that are swallowing your budget. Be careful and mindful that, as a rule, 15- 25% of all ad spend on Google and Facebook is wasted by bots and fraudulent clicks (that's a whole other debate). But you need to set some parameters that block these types of placements from scalping your campaigns budgets.

There are some cool tools to do this and automate the process, saving a lot of time and of course budget. A good audience manager will spot these types of behaviours within campaign reporting really quickly and learn how to avoid these mistakes. Unfortunately the 'enthusiastic amateurs' have little chance of spotting this behaviour, as the bots and fraudulent activity behind the harvesting of clicks and therefore customers off the back of your budgets are extremely sophisticated.

I recently encountered a client who had an internal PPC manager who'd convinced his boss that he was pretty much 'the best of the best'. I was challenged to tell them something that they didn't already know. This guy said in a meeting that he knew everything there is to know about Google Ads (now I know that can't be true as I've been at it for over 20 years, using these tools pretty much every day and I don't think I know half of what is in there. You could spend every waking minute in the Google tools and still not learn it all in a lifetime. Let alone the fact that more features are being added day in, day out).

Anyways, I had to laugh when the guy said he knew it all. Two minutes later I'd ascertained that the account in question had been spending on terms that were nothing to do with the business we were reviewing. There were only a handful of negative keywords and the numbers of adjustments were only 44 in the previous 6 months (and this guy said he was all over it).

Campaigns contained broad match and phrase match without any single keyword ads groups and, furthermore, there were no placement exclusions. When discussed with the MD of the business it was easy to demonstrate value in what we were able to provide in terms of coaching and a sounding board for their internal person—as with all professions they say it takes 10,000 hours to become a master and reach the point of unconscious competence.

In Japan there is a level above this called Takumi, where 60,000 hours are required to become a complete master, that's the equivalent of working eight hours a day, 250 days a year for 30 years. If we say that the given date of the internet beginning is 6th August 1991, it therefore has only just been in existence 30 years as of yet, so there cannot be any true masters or 'Takumi' (unless you count people like me that have been referred to as an 'OG of the net' having worked with the internet since it began). I've had a Google Ads account for 20 years and an MCC for managing 19 other businesses ads spend, so I'd like to think I know a good deal of the tools, but I'd by no means consider myself a complete master.

The other fascinating thing about working with Google and the AI, audiences and data is that no two ads professionals would run campaigns the same way. There is no 'off the shelf' pattern to follow, so much of the work comes back to feel, gut, intuition, experience, tapping the hammer in the right place at the right time—a lot of which cannot be taught. The logic can be explained, the results can be monitored, mistakes will be made. Those that learn and evolve their techniques will win, that is why we need audience and insight specialists. Unfortunately as with many technical jobs this is something that only comes with 'doing'. Yes, the theory can be taught and the framework of rules outlined, but imagination and insight are required. Combine these two essential skills and you'll be a lot closer to having consistently improving campaigns and scalable results. I guess what I am saying is Google Ads and particularly YouTube Ads are not a 'paint by numbers' affair, as with most jobs you can learn the basics but putting your own stamp and style onto campaigns is up to you. No two Google Ads professionals' campaigns would look the same, feel free to experiment and learn, don't be afraid of worse than expected results either—they are just another opportunity to gain knowledge of your audience.

If you're reading this and fresh out of university potentially looking at a career in ads, you're great with data and love psychology, then you'll not go far wrong becoming a data scientist working on campaign insights, audience design and profiling. It's not a job that will make you happy if you don't love the numbers and patterns though. Give me a spreadsheet or dashboard, a screen full of numbers I can read it and I love it, but it's developed over years and years. There are quite a few jobs showing up now such as '*Audience Insights and Development Specialist*' and '*Audience and Analytics Manager*' amongst loads of other variants. This is definitely a specialty that is only set to grow over the next few years.

Yes, Google is making it easier and easier for the enthusiastic amateurs and those that 'think they know what they are doing'. Over the next few years, they are going to make it easier and easier to spend for the average advertiser, producing a level of results for those using the basic tools (and by that I don't mean smart campaigns alone), the trick is to know more than the other players and to watch out for those that say they 'know it all'—PAY ATTENTION!

We've already seen an avalanche of so-called experts proclaiming to give you the 'magic silver bullet system' or 'the system that beats all others' for Facebook Ads courses. Those systems don't exist with Google Ads, but no doubt a whole industry is going to spring up of young guns that will show you through their teachings and lessons learned; how to utilise a system that will dominate on Google Ads or YouTube, believe that and you may as well start looking for the flying pigs and little green men.

There is no system, the only solution is to take the time to learn, test, win, lose, develop. The single biggest skill you are going to need is patience—not something that blends well with wanting immediate results. Good luck and avoid those that make promises like the plague.

I realise I'm now mid-rant, but this is where the industry needs a shake-up. Unfortunately, we have a world where those that are buying a service such as PPC don't understand the first thing about it, or very little about how it actually works. Those that are selling it are making promises and professing to be 'the expert you have been looking for', put this combination together and mix in a large dollop of 'there's money to be made here' with the majority of PPC companies taking a percentage of the advertisers spend to run the campaigns, and you create an industry built on lies, smoke and mirrors, ducking and diving and hardly anyone is challenging or questioning.

Those that are honest and transparent tend to finish last, behind those that have made the big promises (followed by the excuses). If you're an advertiser reading this, ask yourself if you are happy with your PPC performance, could it be better? (the answer is always yes), are you dealing with a trustworthy and experienced agency? (well you wouldn't have chosen them in the first place otherwise), or you've been referred by someone else? (maybe a friend or another business)—but did they have the experience to make the judgement? (well of course they did as they are getting results, right?).

The PPC industry lives off the fact that 99% are enthusiastic amateurs. They are using the basic tools and getting an average result for very, very little work. Trust me, most out there will be doing a tenth of the work they tell you they are. Can you blame them? Do you trust them now? Do they come to you with regular ideas and ways to develop your business? I bet you get some lovely reports covered in numbers. The only number you need to worry about is, are you making a profit on what they are doing? Are they even reporting the profit to you? Rant over.

Bottom line is don't stop exploring, there are so many tools available in Google Ads that nobody knows it all. I'm still learning every day and I encourage you to as well.

Get deep in the weeds, have fun with it, nothing is wrong to test. However, don't be lazy, you're going to get great results with YouTube advertising, but you end up always wanting more.

Don't be that 'set and forget' person who gets a client and sets them up, leaves them on retainer and waits till they moan about the results only then to make some adjustments—that's not fair on the client. There's a healthy chunk of people out there like that. Yes, your client may not appreciate everything you do but you'll know you're doing the right thing and the best job you can for their business.

Yes, clients will come and go, some will go even though you've done a fantastic job… don't sweat it, you don't know their actual reasons for leaving and move on, don't take it personally. I think it's a great career path, but then again, I'm a nerd who loves the numbers and gets a kick out of showing clients results, it doesn't always work, if you're a fellow Google Ads pro I hope you feel the same way, if you're just at the beginning know that you'll never stop learning—if you want to!

Remember though, you've got to love the game to play it well. ▮▮

# ▶| What Google knows about you | Simon

## Google knows EVERYTHING about you and who you are

▶ Have you ever sat in your car and talked about a product, something you have never bought before, and the next day seen ads for that very same product? Obviously, our devices are listening, how that works with privacy laws I don't know! These things are only going to get more prevalent in a good or bad way (depending how you look at it).

Have a look at WhatsApp, what's that all about? It's free to use, it has more than a billion users worldwide and is owned by Facebook, it's not a stretch to imagine that the sole purpose of WhatsApp is to harvest marketing information and data on its users in an effort to secure more advertising revenue for 'the beast' which is Facebook.

At the point of writing many big brands have began boycotting Facebook because of the perpetuation of hate that the platform allows. Facebook has little or no morals, it will claim to 'keep it clean', but on the other hand, it will make no real sustained effort to remove fake news, fraudulent adverts, schemes, racial posts, political influence and other such negativity.

The facts are that it's impossible for Facebook to moderate the content posted onto it. What one person finds offensive, another loves and shares. If moderation were introduced then the shit storm of all shit storms would ensue and the platform would close, pretty much overnight, so therefore, it is impossible to moderate effectively.

YouTube on the other hand has a 'zero tolerance' policy. YouTube employs 10s of thousands of in-house moderators, along with allowing the community to actively moderate the content and has done from early doors. Facebook cannot, as explained, ever hope to have this type of community moderation model. Yes it does 'try' but its tools are hidden away too deep with the obvious intention not to be found or used.

Okay, so debating the difference between each social network could go on forever, but in my opinion, the fundamental difference is that content on channels such as Facebook, is fleeting, there and gone, YouTube you upload a video and it is there in search or on your channel forever as it stands, this builds community better and long-term content into search.

As we go through the next few pages, you'll see the ways you can ensure your privacy and how not to fall into their traps.

### They are ALL listening—is that right, or fair?

- ▶ Are there bots or AI listening to me everywhere I go?
- ▶ Why is Amazon so big and was it designed that way?
- ▶ Are Google or Facebook going to go away?
- ▶ Do I care if my life is being influenced significantly by outside forces?

Maybe you care about some, all, or none of the above. Personally, I care that we are all being enormously influenced by the content we consume online and particularly that on social media. We are looking at generations spending more and more time online, and younger generations that know nothing different.

The challenge is to understand how much influence is being impaired, there is so much data and information out there, literally we are all drowning in information. Harvesting our responses to this barrage of information, news, products, opinions and so forth, is that AI and its level of understanding is increasing exponentially.

Maybe some of the biggest problems will come because everyone is becoming conditioned to getting immediate gratification with likes, shares, comments and views. Where does this all end up?

Is it fair that we are being controlled, listened to and influenced, how will the world change—who knows? I just wanted to throw that out there for you to think about and show you how much control and access to your data these networks have.

It is these systems we have access to with the backend of Google Ads. The same is true with Facebook, that's before we get into Instagram, Twitter, Snapchat, TikTok, LinkedIn, YouTube and so many others.

The tools are literally incredible, the ability to overlay audiences, keywords, topics, app visitors, demographics, time of day, watch through percentages and much more. Behind all that and the other 1,000+ possible combinations within those audiences and that monster piece of big data continues to grow.

Google is continuing to pay agencies like mine and developers to build plugins that work with the Google Ads AI and share a percentage of ad spend—they do this clearly, so that their own system can learn more and more, so that they can have an army of developers, a team of recruiters, evangelists, analysts, data insight pros and of course customers.

Those customers only stick if they achieve a return on investment, the networks have effectively become a monopoly. That means they need to continue to control their customers (the social media and search users, in other words, pretty much everybody). You see where I am going with this?

The whole idea that we, as advertisers, have all these tools available to us and only use a fraction of them baffles me. We are still fighting the system to some extent, Google is giving us the perfect opportunity to work with its AI, as does Facebook, yet I still see many agencies and clients not using the conversion events tracking properly. Please, if you get one thing out of this book, build all your campaigns with multi-level tracking. Track as many conceivably valuable conversion events as you possibly can—show what is valuable to Google and it will reward you.

As an example, we recently took on a new client and they had never run any YouTube Ads before. They are an eCommerce brand, a really big brand with a global offering. Having never run ads before we started off with a conversion event of 'time on site greater than 30 seconds' (if you don't know how to set that up search 'setting up a timer in Google Tag Manager' and you should be good to go). Anyway, the main goal with the initial campaign was to get people onto the site, then to spend time browsing, then adding to cart and finally purchase. What we saw happen was really quite interesting.

In the first week of the campaign, we saw roughly 800 people onto the site, just over 300 staying for 30 seconds (not an unexpected ratio), 70 adding items to the cart, 5 people purchasing. OK, so that doesn't look amazing.

However, this was a completely cold audience and the first test, so not actually disappointing and in fact encouraging as the sales return was 3x on media spend. Had we set out with a goal of just 'sale' as the conversion event we would only have 5 conversions, but as we had over 300 people spending more than 30 seconds onsite, we had decent numbers of achieved conversions, we were teaching Google more quickly.

The next week we found that people who had added items to the cart (70 conversions) had spent an average of 5+ minutes on the site, so now we wanted to change the initial conversion to 'time on site over 3 minutes' therefore moving away from the 30 second model. The campaign did far better in week 2 with a greater number of longer visits, less bounce and Google was finding us more people like the ones who would add to cart.

Yes, eventually we could move to the 'sale' as the main conversion, but hopefully you can now see that by developing and tracking properly you can teach Google (it will love this) and it will give you an enormous advantage if you work like this with your campaigns.

Work that AI!

## Your privacy and the aluminium helmet brigade

What is the 'aluminium helmet brigade'? Well, I'm not talking about the Yugoslavian Fire Service, who happen to have aluminium helmets (perhaps they know something and are keeping a secret). No, I'm talking about those people in society who really don't like their digital footprint being tracked.

The story starts about 4 years ago. I was working in our offices and a call came from the centre manager asking if I could pop up and help with their broadband, as they just couldn't get it working.

I went up to the offices and everyone was sitting there not working, no broadband, long story short, I rebooted the router and switched it to a new channel and got it working, much to the disappointment of one young man whose desk was right over in the corner away from everyone else.

I could see his discomfort and the office manager whispered to me,

*"He's not happy now."*

Following a short conversation out of earshot of this guy, I was informed that:

*"Dave doesn't like WiFi. He feels like everyone will get cancer from the signals coming out of the router, hence why he has stationed himself over in the corner..."*

Obviously, we all know the world doesn't work like that, does it? I went down to my office to test a theory and returned with my Nighthawk router (you know the ones with 5 great big aerials and looks like an alien spaceship). Dave shifted uneasily in his seat as I held the router aloft proudly proclaiming:

*"Look at this bad boy, this can broadcast a signal up to 500 yards, you need to get one of these for your offices."*

Now I know this is cruel, but I've always been up for a bit of fun, so I walked over toward Dave's workstation and placed the router on the windowsill next to him reiterating that,

*"You'll get the best signal distribution from over here, so it can bounce around. As it stands this is probably the spot in the room where all the signals concentrate anyway..."*

Dave stood up, walked out... probably off to the toilets. It was then explained to me that he doesn't even have a mobile phone! Oh dear, I had to apologise to the business owner when I later found out that Dave had to have his desk relocated... I did chuckle a little if I'm honest. During the apology I had said that he should get himself an 'aluminium helmet' and maybe that would offer some comfort and 'protection'. Apparently, he doesn't even like to use email or sign-up for any online services, nor has ever bought anything online. WOW! These people exist and are among us!

The point of this part of the story, should we all be a bit more like 'Dave'?

Think about that for a minute. We are all being tracked and manipulated. Do you care? Well, if we were more Dave then we'd be served up less information that we're interested in and more dross, so does it matter? We are all being influenced by everything on social media.

Okay, the point of advertising is of course to influence someone into purchasing or educate them and 'warm them up' for a future engagement. As I write this, a news story just popped up on the TV about the UK government wanting to implement legislation in order to stop any 'anti-vaccine' stories being posted on social media (it's November 2020 and the vaccine has just been announced for Covid-19), is that fair? Maybe?

One presenter literally just said,

"*Well, there is no vaccine for stupidity*", meaning that anyone who doesn't take the vaccine must be stupid.

Every interaction we have with the world influences us, of course, but is social media going too far? In my opinion, if we allow this type of legislation to be brought forward then we may as well ban social media completely as nobody will be allowed to express their opinions.

We do, though, need to take a step back and not react immediately or impulsively, sharing, liking, commenting on anything that we feel goes against our own personal beliefs, as we are simply magnifying the message we were opposed to in the first place. Where does this all end up? Banning the mention of the colour green? Who knows…?

One of the best uses of social media is of course education.

Educating your listeners/viewers/readers while solving their problems is the go-to of most decent advertising campaigns on social media, especially on YouTube. As an example, one of the most productive campaigns we have worked on recently, ran amazingly well, once we included the education piece. It was for a cosmetic procedure. The initial awareness went out through YouTube, as things turned out, that didn't produce very many results for the client (education phase), those people who watched the first video enabled the audiences to be further refined as we could see how the different demographics were reacting to the content (campaign learning).

More of the ideal audience were added (audience optimisation), next a further video was shown to those that had watched more than 50% of the original video (warm up and deeper education) while more of the optimised audience were added to see video 1.

Hopefully you can see here how advertising spend is optimised, the further people move through a series of videos the more they learn, the less we spend as the audience size reduces the further down the funnel they go.

Once someone hits the third video OR they are seen to have visited the client's website they are then 'made an offer'—that offer as it turned out was a 50% off their first treatment, it was at this point the sales really took off for the client.

Remember that Google is changing the way we remember facts. That's true for all social media and digital marketing, see it, see it again, take it in, it must therefore be true?

As demonstrated, we can observe a group of people in society, who would never see or would never have been exposed to this or any other form of digital advertising campaign, the 'Dave's' of the world. This is clearly an extreme example at one end of the spectrum (in western culture anyway, as thankfully there are still people on this Earth who don't even know what the internet is), but there must be everything and everyone in-between.

My point, ask yourself where you sit and do you choose to be influenced not just by adverts but by every post you see on social media? We are all being influenced and perhaps to some extent controlled subconsciously. Society is becoming driven by likes and immediate gratification. I'm lucky enough to have grown up without access to the internet or social media in my formative years, young people today have no such luxury, they know no different. It has always been there to some extent, yes there is no stopping it, but we can all make a choice to be a little more like Dave can't we?

This book concerns itself mainly with the benefits of advertising, talking about the tools around YouTube and other digital channels that can help advertisers think and plan.

Why, therefore, am I seemingly bemoaning the way social media is transforming the way people and society think and act as a whole?

Purely so those of you that read this may get to thinking a little deeper about how your audiences perceive your content and you can use that knowledge. We are seeing a change in advertising online where even the account managers and those running their own campaigns expect results straight off the bat without educating their audiences, or thinking carefully about their emotional responses. That can't be a good thing.

Nothing, no advert, however good, beats a brilliant funnel, good landing pages, user experience, interesting videos with well written scripts and perfectly crafted audiences. Sequencing, tracking, learning, reiteration, testing, offers, emotion, creativity… all of these things have to line up to deliver great results, remember that.

Ask yourself, how would you like to be marketed to?

## Fraud and Google—Clicks from bots and other scandalous underhand practices

'Back in the day' (in the late 90s), people were making millions of dollars off the back of Google AdSense; where if you are a website owner you publish ads from the display network onto your site and when someone clicks, you share the revenue Google earns from the advertiser. The classic example being 'money sites' that were created purely with this intention. We've all seen them, you click an article title, picture of something interesting or a link from a blog etc. You then end up on a website that is not a website, by that I mean a site FULL OF ADS, it looks like a website but there is pretty much nothing there apart from more links and ads.

As an example, I could set up '*Simon's Casino*' and the people that land on it are served further ads to 888 Poker, William Hill, Mega Bingo etc. filling my own 'money site' with AdSense then allows me to concentrate on just building traffic and links to the site (and watching the revenue grow). Before quite a few of the Google SEO updates, these types of sites were far more prevalent as there was a whole industry built around them and ranking them in search.

Google eventually cottoned on and today, thankfully, these types of sites are far less prominent, although they still do pop up with their traffic coming from social, blogs and fake news. The scandal here revolves around the fact that Google frankly doesn't care where the clicks are coming from as long as they are getting paid. Yes, they do care about retention and customer experience (we are the customers when searching), but the bottom line is if there is a click on a paid piece of collateral be that a link, display, PPC or YouTube advert they get paid and so do the publishers/creators.

Obviously, now if you take YouTube in isolation, we are in the early stages of adoption. Still, advertisers are using a 'spray and pray' approach as if the viewer skips then the advertiser doesn't always pay (depending on the campaign type). Many thousands of influencers are making millions off the back of YouTube with revenue shares from YouTube/Google and sponsorship deals, plus product placements. There's still a long way to go and YouTube is ever evolving, as advertisers learn to shape and define audiences more carefully to those that suit their campaigns.

If we look back into the annals of time, well as far back as 2016, i.e. 'the stone age' in terms of the internet compared to today. There's the case of a bunch of Russian hackers, and probably one of the biggest fraud cases of all time (I'm doing them a disservice as this was an extremely well planned, organised and executed attack). They were purportedly making between 3 and 5 million dollars a DAY from Google Ads, stealing from advertisers right under Google's nose and there was literally nothing anyone could do to stop it, should Google have spotted it?

In an audacious fraud, the scammers were at its peak running over a quarter of a million different URLs and somewhere in the region of half a million bots, located across multiple data centres, across the world. The bots were tasked with watching video and by utilising fake domains, they could trick the AI into choosing their websites to place adverts and pay for ads space. Google therefore thought that their 'high traffic' sites were valuable and placed lots of advertiser's collateral there, the revenue from the advertisers being split with Google and the fraudsters.

Once a fraudulent site had established itself as an authority, the algorithm then chose more and more advertisers who were prepared to bid higher and higher for the space, bigger brands, more money, higher revenue for the fraudsters; an ever-fulfilling prophecy of doom for the advertisers. As a caveat if you are running your campaigns properly then it's possible to exclude these types of placements as you would not be seeing conversion events (not the valuable ones anyways).

What became known as the Methbot attack, these fraudsters bots 'fake watched' 100s of millions of video views every day, and when you look at the facts, where they were driving an average of over $10 a thousand views in revenue for themselves, it's easy to see how they could make such eye watering amounts of money every single day. And that was back in 2015-16.

They were even having their clever bot army take actions, clicks, browsing, completely faking the actions real people take when browsing sites. Going so far as to create massive numbers of social media profiles and populating them with fake pictures, stories, it all looked real, well real enough!

Security firm 'White Ops' dubbed the Russian hack by AFK13 (Ad Fraud Komanda) and having faked domains they executed what could possibly be the biggest internet fraud of all time. Some of the world's biggest brands had their sites copied so that it appeared the ads were on completely legitimate sites, but it really was pretty much just the bots doing all the work! Couple that with millions of IP addresses that looked for all intensive purposes as far as Google was concerned that were located in US residential areas and you have a perfect storm, or conditions for fraud.

What caught my attention though was the statement that Eddie Schwartz, Chief Operating Officer at White Ops made. Besides the fact that they had proof this was going on (they wouldn't reveal their methods but were confident that the hack was Russian), White Ops said that *"Historically...it's been challenging to get cooperation with Russia to prosecute cyber-related crimes."* (strange that) and that *"It had passed the information to law enforcement..."* who knows what happened there.

Geir Magnusson, an ad fraud expert and CTO at Sourcepoint Technologies, stated it should be possible to shut AFK13 out of the ad market:

*"All actors in a bidding ecosystem are known and have contractual business relationships—this isn't a 'dark web' of anonymous buyers and sellers."*

*"I think the key will be ensuring that information like what White Ops has found gets broadly disseminated, and that the actors in the ecosystem work closely to help each other 'follow the money' and enforce the shunning of bad actors."*

(Credit to this Forbes article if you want to read it in full—*https:// www.forbes.com/sites/thomasbrewster/2016/12/20/ methbot-biggest-ad-fraud-busted/*)

The takeaway though is the scary fact that if a system exists to allow publishers to garner significant revenue from gaming that same system there are always going to be people trying to exploit it.

## The Poachers Turned Gamekeepers

It has, very recently, become more obvious that individuals such as Mark Zuckerberg have tried to soften their stance and head towards the *'we aren't trying to harvest every last piece of information out of you'* position that they want you to believe. They would have you think that they 'care deeply' about your privacy. They do, but they just invade it with your permission and access to every part of your life! I wouldn't be surprised if there is an 'estimated bank balance' field somewhere locked deep in the algorithm, along with details on your sexual preferences, a propensity to commit a crime index/score, links to suspicious activities and much more. Who knows what the networks all hold on us now.

Every step that these companies take, into saying they are protecting your privacy they take another into the *'stopping anyone else from accessing your data like we do' tec*h—think about it for a while, why would Facebook, Amazon, Google etc. allow anyone else to join their exclusive club?

Mr. Bezos is the king here, his algorithm and tech were the building blocks on which all the data harvesting was, and is built. It was a great ambition of his to fully understand and map purchasing behaviours, plus build possibly the greatest UX of all time. He and his team have gone on to create the largest company in the world, but now they are there at the top of the table they certainly aren't admitting any more members. Those that do 'invent' anything tech or AI that could challenge that are swiftly snapped up and purchased by these behemoths or dispatched as if they were a freshly caught salmon on the banks of the Tay.

Recently we saw ITP take hold with Apple saying it was *'limiting Safari cookie lifespan to 24 hours'*. Guess which websites most people visit every day and are therefore able to maintain these ever so 'essential' first party cookies? Laughable isn't it, that the poachers who now claim to be the gamekeepers are actively blocking everyone out of the playground, but at the same time claiming to be whiter than white? What a game they have played, are playing and will continue to do so.

The US Justice Department is slowly moving toward challenging the position of Google in the courts on the basis that they are too large a monopoly, but where does that end? With the state controlling Google, I don't think so, do you?

Advertisers and brands are beholden to these social media and tech giants for data and the ability to monitor, target, assign campaigns for remarketing and work with their audience management tools.

The question I don't have the answer for currently is, *'what will it be like in 10 years time, will advertising agencies even need to or be able to exist'*? The tools are amazing and especially the audience profiling, much is obviously hidden, but in this book, I hope to open up some of the little tricks and tips we use to help you as an advertiser.

I know a lot of what goes on can be seen almost as witchcraft and smoke and mirrors. The point is we have an opportunity as advertisers to use this data and use it wisely, to save, spend and teach the advertising platforms what type of customers we want and those that have intent to buy. My view on the 'closed shop' is purely there to give context and the landscape in which we are all playing and demonstrate that those at the top are making it ever harder to join their club as a placement platform.

Look at all the search engines that have disappeared over the years, glance at Bing now, surviving off the back of its installed base with pretty much all the Windows PCs on earth coming with it loaded as default. It's clear that Microsoft isn't playing in the traditional search game anymore, having given up long ago in its battle against Google.

Ask someone for the verb 'to search' and the answer will be 'Google it', ask yourself what it would take for you to choose a different search engine other than Google? ∎

# ⏭ Some helpful bits and bobs | Andy

## Video production values

▶ When it comes to YouTube we often encounter a barrier with clients.

*"I don't have any video collateral."*

And then they say...

*"Well how much is it to produce some video?"*

Before I answer these and discuss them further, I'd like to frame this section.

Large brands know how much video costs. They know how long it takes and they generally understand the more subtle nuances and investment it takes. Well, in general they do.

Mid-sized companies it depends. Some do understand, some don't.

Smaller businesses, most don't really appreciate the work that goes into it.

There are lots of caveats here of course.

The large brands may have done TV, so have experience.
- Some marketing departments think it can be done super quick and cheap.
- Some smaller businesses think it costs hundreds of thousands and a need to work with massive crews.
- Some think it can be done for £50 with some off-the-shelf animation.
- Some think it needs to be super high quality and Steven Spielberg-esq.
- Some think it can be done on your phone and is fine all wobbly.

The real answer is 'all of the above' because it simply depends on context.
- Where is it going?
- Who is the target market?
- What are you trying to achieve?
- What is your tone of voice?
- What action/takeout do you want the consumer to do/feel?
- And finally, what are your brand values?

Because all of that drives the creative.

You see, it might be right that you film secretly on a dodgy old phone as if it's 'spy-like'.

That would be the right thing to do if the idea is about secretly filming your neighbour because you might be thinking he's dealing drugs. It could be for a Police Crime Prevention campaign.

Equally it might be highly stylised and beautifully filmed with loads of lights, models wearing stunning dresses because it's for a wedding brand.

So, it is all about context.

One of my favourite ads used a breakdown camera on a motorway. It was for VW. The car towed the tow truck that had broken down. Simply, stunning. Yet it was filmed terribly BECAUSE it was the right thing to do for the idea and what needed to be communicated.

If you think you require full blown production or are not sure where to start, ask for advice from a professional filming production company, it doesn't always cost as much as you think.

But if you are filming some simple videos here are a few tips for 'made at home' style:

**Use Plenty of Light.**

If you can, use 'God's light' as we used to say on shoot. That is natural light. It makes a huge difference in the quality of a video.

When outdoors, try to get your footage in the morning or evening, when the light is softer. Midday light (laser light) coming from straight overhead can cause harsh shadows on your subjects if the sun is bright, whilst morning and evening light is more workable, and can be more visually appealing, if you know how to work it with a bit of practice.

If you do have to film in the middle of the day, try doing it on a cloudy day, but not too cloudy as it can be dark. Light cloud cover gives you a nice natural light and on any subject the shadows are perfect. In many ways better than sunlight. Alternatively, find a shady area under trees for more dappled light.

Filming indoors has its own challenges. Try to avoid overhead lighting—it can cast unflattering shadows on your subjects' faces, a bit like overhead sun. It's just harsh and clumsy. Windows are the natural light source but make sure the subject is facing the light and not filming against the window otherwise they will be in harsh shadow. You can also use a large lamp or two to cast the type of light you want.

But consider the effect you want to create in your finished video. Do you want your subject's face entirely lit up or do you want some shadows? This very much depends on what creative look and feel you are trying to achieve.

I love heavy and dramatic lighting, both indoors and outdoors, but it's not right for everything. Using lots of shadow looks intense, but it can be distracting in videos where drama isn't the intended effect. If you want to use flat light in your video, then balance light sources on either side of the camera. You can place them either behind the camera or just in front of it. My only caveat is that it can look, well, flat. And a bit dull.

Another good tip is to use large pieces of white card to bounce light back into the subject, as this can create a nice light and shade. A decent light reflector starts at less than £10 and is well worth the price, if video is something you are considering taking seriously.

As a side, you can buy good quality lights that have decent quality settings for around £200.

**Use a Clean Background.**

The background you use for filming is key. Avoid messy or distracting backgrounds, however, again it can depend on the story you are trying to communicate. If it's to do with busy shopping, lots of people in the background may be right. But if it's a close up of you talking about an in-depth subject then maybe simpler is better.

One easy way to get a professional look for your video is to use a solid-coloured background.

Beware though, this can look like a green screen mistake and a bit boring. If you can dress it simple that can help. A plant, a picture, makes such a difference in my opinion to just flatness.

A wall, or a large sheet of backdrop paper are all good options. Make sure your subject stands several feet away from the backdrop to avoid casting shadows on it.

If you can shoot your video in a 'professional' environment: the place where you actually work or spend time. You can create professional looking videos in your home office.

Just think about the dressing of the frame. What can you take out or add in so it's not dull, or too much?

**Choose a Good Video Editing Program.**

This all depends on what budget you are working to, and what computer you use. Or even if you know someone who can do it for you. iMovie is good and free on Mac, but more professional options include Final Cut Pro and Adobe Premiere Pro.

You'll also need to consider captioning and subtitling as this helps massively with your videos online. Zubtitle is a good one to try.

Here are the key features to think about:
- The ability to add text
- The ability to trim and crop videos
- The ability to change the aspect ratio
- Adding filters and overlays
- A library of stock videos and sounds

**Keep Your Editing Simple.**

KISS.

Keep it simple, stupid. This goes for everything. The filming, the graphics, and most definitely the edit.

Trying out different effects can be fun, but it will just look crap unless you spend a lot of time researching and practising. Don't go too crazy. A simple, clean editing style generally looks best unless you are a Spielberg in the making.

Things you should be sure to do during the editing stage include:
- Using noise cancelling to clean up any background noise
- Adjusting the lighting balance if scenes are dark or light
- Cutting out awkward pauses and silences or mistakes

**Prioritise Crisp, Clear Audio.**

Audio quality is more important than your video quality. Most people are willing to watch a video that's not shot in HD because we have become accustomed to watching videos on our phones that are homemade.

So grainy, wobbly or whatever is passable as long as everything sounds good!

If the sound is fuzzy, indistinct or crackly, it's enough to make anybody hit the 'skip' button within a few seconds of starting to play a video.

As audio matters so much, buying a good microphone is the first piece of equipment you should invest in. Get the best one you can afford. But if you need an entry level even a LAV mic will do. Search it—less than £20.

It's not so tricky to capture clear audio—put your microphone as close to you or the subject as possible. Simple. Just be aware of any background noise that your microphone might be picking up, like passing traffic, birds etc..

**Avoid Shaky Footage.**

Drunken looking footage will make any video look like a home movie and can make your viewers feel sick. It's impossible to hold a camera completely steady, so use a tripod, or set your camera on a sturdy surface against something, such as a pile of books. A good bit of Gaffer Tape can also work wonders. Equally, if you can invest around £100, a handheld steady camera can be a great investment.

Once you've got your camera set up don't move it! You'll just keep going around in circles.

Just film what you have to do. THEN move it and redo a scene, or the whole lot from a slightly different angle. Then edit together the best bits. But you don't have a crew and proper equipment so it will just look crap, right? Most good editing software lets you move in and to the sides to have a good look and really put together the best bits of what you filmed.

Panning around constantly detracts from the professional look of a video. It's better to cut from one shot to another.

If your footage still turns out shaky, video stabilisation software can help to fix it afterwards. Some cameras also have built-in stabilisation that you can use while you're filming. Slowing down your footage can also help to make shakiness less obvious.

**Understand the Rule of Thirds.**

Please, please just research this.

The rule of thirds is one of the most basic principles of film composition.

Imagine that there's a 3-by-3 grid laid over the field you're filming. Instead of placing your subject right in the middle of the shot (which by the way is OK on occasions), you should place your subject along one of the lines of the grid. The points where the lines intersect are strong areas of focus and draws the viewer's eyes in.

You don't have to follow the rule of thirds all the time but it's a good idea to try to use it as often as possible. As you gain experience, you'll get a better instinct for when to stick with the rule and when to break it.

**Use Your Phone (if appropriate).**

You can use your phone to capture video footage. It's a doddle.

Bentley and BMW have filmed commercials on them, and you can even produce cinema quality on them. Less of a doddle.

My advice would be (because there are so many different phones and cameras with varying quality out there) do a bit of research into your own model.

Some have 4K which is amazing. Some don't. Some of the light sensors are better than others. So again, it's all about research and finding out what's best for you.

It all comes down to context as I said right at the start of this section.

And just try it. Film some stuff. Look at it. Review it. Try again. Keep it simple, don't expect Hollywood and give it a whirl.

**Work on Your Camera Presence.**

This just takes a bit of practice. And trust me, the first ones will not be great, but they will get better. The more you do it the better you get and the more relaxed you become.

The way you carry yourself on camera has an enormous impact on how your content looks. However saying that, nobody got an Oscar the first time around.

Appearing nervous, fidgety, or uncomfortable on camera will distract viewers from your message so find ways to relax. Practice, bin, do again. It won't take long, but whatever you do, don't give in.

Use calm, open body language. Stand up straight—poor posture is immediately obvious on camera. Keep your shoulders back and your muscles relaxed. Don't cross your arms, since this makes you look closed-off. Don't be wooden either. Or a mad hand waving journalist on the BBC. Practice a nice middle ground.

This is a big one. Smile, especially at the beginning and end of your video. It makes a huge difference in how friendly you seem.

Slow down slightly when you talk and make an effort to enunciate clearly. It may feel slow to you but on cameras, a slower pace is good. Use pauses and if you stumble, carry on, this can make you look more authentic.

If you feel jittery, try using props to keep your hands occupied. Having a pen in the hand can give you something to focus on besides the camera. Even holding a cuppa.

Practice, practice, practice. Watch footage of yourself and look at the areas where you could improve. Then have another go!

**Shoot from a Variety of Angles.**

As I mentioned earlier, cutting from one angle to another is a great way to add visual interest to your videos. But be careful to not overdo it.

This is a useful technique if you're making a how-to video, a product demo, or indeed many other types of video that shows you doing something rather than just talking.

I always say shoot plenty of B-roll footage for each video, so you have the option of using it later if you want to. And in my experience these bits of footage are lifesavers for your videos!

Make sure your shifts in perspective are not too small, they don't really create the intended effect—they just look jarring to the viewer.

**Plan Your Videos in Advance.**

The biggest mistake people make is planning.

They simply don't do it.

Before any video or script, ask yourself what you want to achieve or communicate by making this video. Who is it aimed at? Why will they be listening? What do we want them to feel? What actions do we want them to take?

Once you've defined your video's goals, write a script and if possible, a stickman storyboard. Then revise them until they're as good as you can make them. Rearrange, rewrite, and delete sections that don't work. Rambling videos bore viewers, so keep your videos as brief and tight as possible.

Take the time to plan your video really well before you start, ensure that you have thought about the job beforehand: your background, props you use, camera angles, lighting, your script and finally, how you edit your videos. Make notes, even if only simple ones. Get everything ready before. Planning makes it so much easier.

**Promote Your Videos.**

- Creating your videos is only half of it.
- The other half is getting people to watch them.
- And there is a lot written in this book about this subject!
- So, you have done your first video.
- Practice will help. Don't beat yourself up.
- Just go again. And keep going.

The more professional your videos look, the more your business and brand will benefit.

Making professional-looking videos does take practice and in many ways know-how.

By trying it and redoing it you can improve the quality of your next video easily just by applying the basic tricks and tips mentioned here. There's loads of great stuff online too so just have a search.

**The Customer Avatar (or Profile as I prefer)**

Trying to understand our ideal customer isn't an easy task.

Too many times I've heard (some very senior CEOs) say "everyone".

Which is a joke.

The old school way of ABC classification is dead and gone. It simply has not got the depth required in today's modern world. Don't get me wrong, it can give a base start but tread very carefully.

You then have a multitude of terms such as DINKies, Dual Income No kids.

Again, all well and good, but it is only the surface in my opinion.

As I've mentioned in other parts of this book, understanding your customer or potential customer is key. However, doing it on a broad-brush stroke, marketeers' level, sometimes makes the science overrun the human element.

In reality you need both. We need the data side, but we need the empathy and understanding side. This is crucial so the creative is emotionally connecting, and the targeting is laser-like to their hopes, fear, desires and dreams.

But let's start with some basics.

## Definition of target audience

Let's start with the definition. What is the target audience? Basically—your potential customers. It's a group of people who you think may like your products or services. It can be described by behavioural and demographic attributes, such as age, gender, income, education or localisation. According to Yahoo, 54% of customers find personalised ads to be more engaging and McKinsey shows that ads tailored to client's needs can significantly increase ROI—up to 8 times, and lift sales of at least 10% in fact!

So, finding the right audience is crucial for your campaigns' efficiency.

## Types of target audience

There are a lot of techniques and ways that can be used in finding your right audience. As I've said, age, income, education, gender are just a few examples. Some of the key things to consider are:

**Demographic:** Socio-economic data that describes a user. This group includes attributes, such as age, income, education, gender or geographic location. Using demographic data, you can target your campaign, for example at young people, aged 18-24, both female and male from towns with a population larger than 20,000.

**Interests:** This is data about users' hobbies, passions, things that they are looking for and reading about. It can be anything from books to movies, music, cars, marketing, parenting or dance. By knowing your customers' passions, you gain powerful knowledge because you know how to engage your clients and what products/services will be interesting for them.

**Purchase intentions:** Data is crucial, especially for eCommerce. Audiences are divided into groups of users who recently looked for a specific product, such as a laptop, refrigerator or car and did not look for it previously. It means that they want to buy a new thing, but first need to gain more knowledge about the demanded product.

When it comes to defining your customer targeting purposes, you can use just one type of audience attribute (e.g. demography) or mix all of them to create a detailed target group and reach out to them precisely. In other words, marketers can reach out to groups of users: age 35-42, interested in cars, who are going to buy a new vehicle.

Try to truly understand your audience. What are their problems and needs? Who are they? Start from your current customer base—what attributes do they have? If you store data about users, start analysing it by using adequate tools, such as Google Analytics or *Data Management Platform*. It will give you a lot of insights into your clients' profiles.

You should also analyse your products and services. What benefits do you offer? Try to list them. Then think about people who have a need that your benefit fulfils.
- How old are they?
- What are they interested in?
- What are they looking for and why does your product meet their needs?

It will help you to find the right attributes of your target group.

Finally, experiment. Build basic, standard segments and use them in your campaign to check how they perform. Next, try to create a new segment, add a non-obvious attribute, build audiences based on how much they spend and offer them products that they can afford to buy.

Understanding your audience, what they are looking for and what they truly need is a challenging piece of work. Analyse what they do, offer them personalised brand experience and measure the results. Building the right audience is not a single activity—to increase the sales you need to review your target audiences and check how their expectations change over time.

All these things are quite practical, but there is one thing I would also encourage alongside all this work. An actual avatar (profile).

Why?

Because it feels deeper and more personal and can get you thinking like them. It also helps when it comes to casting for any videos! In short it allows us more understanding, more empathy and makes us, ultimately, more emotionally connected to them and their lives.

So, who is your ideal customer?

Take a moment to think about your business, and who you would really love to see walking in the door, visiting your website, signing up and at the end of the day buying!

And so here is the need for the *ideal customer avatar (profile)*.

Probably the best way a business can decide upon their target audience is by coming up with an *ideal customer avatar (profile)* because it's highly effective.

It's simply a detailed profile of your ideal customer. It doesn't make assumptions or categorise people into groups such as ABC, or DINKies. The avatar focuses on one person (or couple, or family) and details everything about them. It goes into much greater depth. Explore everything, the car they drive, the holidays they take, their struggles, their likes, their dislikes, favourite shows, books. What they drink. What their social time looks like. Their jobs.

EVERYTHING.

You don't really create an avatar, you discover it. And thereby you discover your ideal customer.

But maybe you have to do several to cover all bases.

And one tip, think of someone you know who would be an ideal customer. This way you can be more detailed as you'll know them. Get the client to work with you also, it's a great way to build rapport and better understanding all round. ∎